PRAISE FOR *TO BE A BETTER COACH*

"*To Be a Better Coach* is one of those books that has something for everyone, from the novice to the experienced coach, coach educator, and parent alike. The 'In Action' sections and 'Coaching Tips' provide an immediate application of the concept(s) for coaching practice. Authentic scenarios and examples support the literature throughout the book that any coach will be able to relate to. *To Be a Better Coach* will not only make you a better coach, it will help you be a better person."
—**Ronald W. Quinn, Ed.D., associate professor and program director, Coaching Education & Athlete Development, Xavier University**

"*To Be a Better Coach* is a must read for all prospective coaches interested in working in youth sports. The authors provide a well-researched, detailed, enjoyable, and action-oriented resource that serves as a great reminder about the responsibility that all coaches have to inspire, educate, develop, and care for their athletes in the healthiest and safest way possible."
—**Shay Boyle, President, Notre Dame College Prep, Niles, IL; former NCAA D1/D2 assistant college basketball coach**

"*To Be a Better Coach* is a blueprint for coaches on how to create a successful environment for your athletes and program. It is very detail oriented but also an easy-to-read resource for coaches just starting out or veteran coaches who are hoping to improve their approach and program. *To Be a Better Coach* is a must read for all coaches!"
—**Melissa Volk, head girls hockey coach, Andover High School, Andover, MN, 2020 State 2A Champions**

"*To Be a Better Coach* does a great job setting the structure and framework every coach needs to improve their ability to coach athletes in today's culture. The authors show there is more than Xs and Os if you want to be your best as a coach."
—**Dennis Hopkins, CAA; director of athletics; head coach, varsity boys basketball, Oakland Christian School, Auburn Hills, MI**

"*To Be a Better Coach* is both an extremely practical and deeply philosophical approach to working with young developing athletes in any sport. Being both a head coach and employer of close to a dozen other part-time coaches, I would absolutely use this systematic and thoughtful pedagogy to create a team culture where athletes and coaches strive to get better every day in a safe, mindful, and uplifting fashion."
—**Mark J. Sowa, head coach and owner, Vandal Aquatic Club, LLC, Moscow, Idaho/Spokane, WA**

"Pete Van Mullem and Lori Gano-Overway's dedication to quality youth sports shows as the authors delve into all of the key aspects of what makes a great coach. *To Be a Better Coach* provides engaging exercises, real-world scenarios and research-backed advice to encourage coaches to improve at their craft. No matter your role in sports, we can all agree that the impact of a coach on a young athlete's experience is unparalleled. This book helps us strive toward better youth sports for kids through better coaching."
—**Kate Nematollahi, director of education programs, National Alliance for Youth Sports**

"Pete Van Mullem and Lori Gano-Overway have taken decades of knowledge . . . and provided a well-thought-out game plan for new and continually evolving coaches. Their approach in teaching coaches the responsibility of being a holistic, big-picture, and life-lesson impactor will serve as a valuable foundation for coaches passionate about the success of their athletes during competition and beyond."
—**Heather Stewart, USA Basketball regional coordinator, Positive Coaching Alliance Certified Trainer, Golden State Warriors Basketball Academy Coach**

"This publication provides much needed practical guidance and important considerations for those working with youth athletes. The authors incorporate solid theory about effective coaching and youth development as they move quickly into specific examples and detailed descriptions of application in a variety of settings. These examples will keep the reader focused on how to achieve the multiple goals that coaches should attend to as they work with our young people."
—**Sara Lopez, co-director for the Center for Leadership in Athletics and executive director for the Intercollegiate Athletic Leadership (IAL) M.Ed. program, University of Washington**

To Be a
Better Coach

PROFESSIONAL DEVELOPMENT IN SPORT COACHING

Published in partnership with the United States Center for Coaching Excellence

Series Editor: Karen Collins

This book series provides coaches, sport organization leaders, directors of coaching, educators, and athletic directors with the skills, guidelines, and research-based best practices to support quality coach development. Offering practical, readily-implemented information, these books will help to improve coaching performance across multiple sport contexts.

To Be a Better Coach

A Guide for the Youth Sport Coach and Coach Developer

PETE VAN MULLEM AND LORI GANO-OVERWAY

ROWMAN & LITTLEFIELD
Lanham • Boulder • New York • London

Published by Rowman & Littlefield
An imprint of The Rowman & Littlefield Publishing Group, Inc.
4501 Forbes Boulevard, Suite 200, Lanham, Maryland 20706
www.rowman.com

6 Tinworth Street, London, SE11 5AL, United Kingdom

British Library Cataloguing in Publication Information Available

Library of Congress Cataloging-in-Publication Data

Names: Mullem, Pete Van, author. | Gano-Overway, Lori A., author.
Title: To be a better coach : a guide for the youth sport coach and coach
    developer / Pete Van Mullem and Lori Gano-Overway.
Description: Lanham, Maryland : Rowman & Littlefield, 2021. | Series:
    Professional development in sport coaching | Includes bibliographical
    references and index. | Summary: "This book combines comprehensive
    research in coach development and hands-on experience to offer coaches
    and coach developers concrete, practical suggestions to improve coaching
    performance in youth sport. It speaks directly to coaches working in
    community youth sport programs, interscholastic sport, and private youth
    sport organizations." —Provided by publisher.
Identifiers: LCCN 2020056418 (print) | LCCN 2020056419 (ebook) | ISBN
    9781538141977 (paperback) | ISBN 9781538141984 (ebook)
Subjects: LCSH: Sports for children—Coaching.
Classification: LCC GV709.24 .M85 2021 (print) | LCC GV709.24 (ebook) |
    DDC 796.083—dc23
LC record available at https://lccn.loc.gov/2020056418
LC ebook record available at https://lccn.loc.gov/2020056419

♾™ The paper used in this publication meets the minimum requirements of
American National Standard for Information Sciences—Permanence of Paper
for Printed Library Materials, ANSI/NISO Z39.48-1992.

Contents

Foreword

As a young coach, I was always searching for materials to help me become a better coach. I searched out books that would give me not only information to make my team better on the court but would help me working with players off the court as well. *To Be a Better Coach* is this kind of resource, an all-inclusive source of information to help you improve as a coach. Coaches expect their players to improve their game. In order for your players to get better, coaches must improve and become lifelong learners. *To Be a Better Coach* is a must for any coach.

To Be a Better Coach closely aligns with the USA Basketball curriculum. USA Basketball is the governing body for all basketball in the United States. *To Be a Better Coach* will provide coaches information they need to improve their coaching DNA. The five qualities that make up outstanding coaches' DNA, according to USA Basketball, are teaching, authenticity, adaptability, organization, and humility.

To Be a Better Coach also includes information coaches can apply directly in practice as it relates to the USA Basketball curriculum, such as the best way to build a culture in your program, building relationships with players and parents, and organizing your practice sessions.

I highly recommend this book for all youth coaches! Coaching is a profession that will affect more lives in one year than most professions affect in a lifetime.

Don Showalter
Coach Director, Youth Division
U16-17 National Team Men's Coach 2009–2018
Ten-Time Gold Medalist
USA Basketball

Introduction

Coaches play an important role in the lives of athletes, often becoming a leader in sport organizations and within the local community. Coaches help others reach their potential by understanding the core coaching responsibilities and the underlying knowledge, skills, and behaviors to fulfill their role as a coach. However, becoming this type of coach does not happen after coaching a single season, reading a book, or taking a series of courses. Rather, it is a lifelong endeavor. This book is meant to help coaches in this lifelong journey by outlining some best practices associated with core coaching responsibilities and highlighting how they could be used in coaching practice. In doing so, the book also serves as a resource for coach developers to use in facilitating coach development with their youth sport coaches. This book begins by setting the context in which youth coaches work and describes who the stakeholders are in youth sport, outlines the typical path to become a youth sport coach, and, finally, shares what youth coaches should know and do to meet their core coaching responsibilities.

THE YOUTH SPORT SETTING

Youth sport experiences vary for youth ages 6 to 18 across recreational and competitive settings, including community parks and recreation youth programs, sport club programs, youth sport travel teams, and private training facilities. Figure I.1 depicts the diverse nature of youth sport, highlighting the

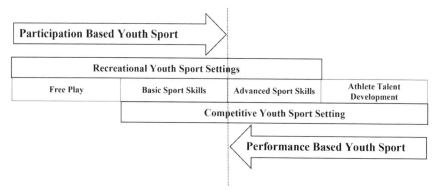

FIGURE I.1
Participation/Performance Continuum

overlap of recreational and competitive settings relative to participation- and performance-based youth sport. Participation-based youth sport programs are dedicated to developing basic sport skills, creating a joy for engaging in physical activity and building confidence for continued long-term participation in sport activities.[1] Participation-focused youth sport programs are often found in a recreational sport setting, such as municipal parks and recreation programs or through nonprofit youth organizations that provide supervised open facilities, such as the Boys & Girls Clubs of America. The participation-based program is designed to provide opportunities for youth in local communities to play and learn sport skills regardless of socioeconomic status or skill level. While not ideal, the coach of a participation-based community youth program is often a parent volunteer, or the organization may offer programming that does not include a coach for each team. In this setting, coaches may or may not have experience with the particular sport they are coaching.

Performance-based youth sport focuses on intensive preparation in developing sport skills with the intent to achieve success in a competitive setting.[2] Performance-based youth sport in the United States often takes the form of a youth sport travel team, club sport program, or private training academies. These programs are designed to develop advanced sport skills and athletic talent development. Youth are selected to participate based on age level, current skill level, and/or their potential for athletic development.[3] In addition, opportunities for youth within clubs, travel teams, and private training academies may be limited by socioeconomic status[4] and/or the social status of their parents in the community.[5]

Youth sport clubs and travel teams are often coached by the parents of one or more of the players on the team, on a volunteer basis. The requirements for these coaches are limited and may require a background check. However, some club and travel programs, especially those that provide individual skill development training, may employ a part-time or full-time coach. An established club sport program, with paid coaches, may require additional training beyond a background check. It is important to note that there is a lot of variability in travel and club sport at the youth level in regard to how coaches are trained and what the specific training is required of the coach.

Scholastic, or school-sponsored, sport programs for youth include both participation- and performance-based sport. That is, they provide opportunities to participate and learn basic sport skills at earlier school levels (e.g., sixth–ninth grade) while also devoting time to develop more advanced sport skills, athletic development, and competing against other schools at later school levels (e.g., tenth–twelfth grade). Further, scholastic sport is designed to enhance the educational experience that students receive in the classroom.[6] In scholastic sport, middle schools and junior high schools tend to provide more participation-focused sport experiences than high schools by implementing no-cut policies and equal playing time. However, school districts have the option to structure high school sport programs in a manner they determine is best for their schools and community,[7] which means the scholastic sport experience for adolescents in one community may be different from a neighboring community. Scholastic sport is also referred to as interscholastic sport.

The requirements to coach school-sponsored sports are outlined by each school district and fall under the guidance of each state's high school activities association. Common requirements for the scholastic coach include a background check and basic coach education in the form of a workshop or training session on coaching principles. Basic coach education also includes safety instruction, such as concussion awareness training, CPR and first aid certification, and risk management procedures. The scholastic sport coach is often paid with a stipend or as part of his or her contractual obligations as a teacher in the school district.

Privatized youth sport programs may also include both participation- and performance-based sport. In this type of setting, the organization operates like a business where the client is the youth athlete. The expected outcome is demonstrated improved performance specific to program focus. For example, a youth sport soccer club might manage soccer teams across multiple age levels in boys' and girls' soccer within the community. The younger athletes participate in a structured play environment learning basic sport skills, agility, and life skills with no competition, while older athletes may be working on advanced sport skills, agility, stamina, strength, and/or mental preparation and competing at a high level. However, other private youth sport organizations, like elite sport academies, may be exclusively performance-based sport programs that provide sport-specific training and competitive opportunities for athletes. The requirements to be employed in an elite sport academy may include specific training and/or certification relative to the sport or services offered by the business. For example, a coach may have training as a certified strength coach (CSC). A coach working for an elite sport academy is often employed either part time or full time.

Each of the previously described youth sport settings include a variety of stakeholders, each playing a role in the quality of the youth sport program. A brief definition of each stakeholder is provided as it relates to youth sport.

Coach developer: Any trained individual responsible for providing coach development activities for coaches under their guidance.[8] While coach developers are trained to provide resources, advice, and encouragement to coaches by facilitating coach learning, assessing coaches, and mentoring coaches, some individuals, either trained or untrained, may informally engage in the duties of the coach developer. For example, youth program directors, athletic directors, and private sport training facility owners/managers all could have coach development responsibilities in addition to the other essential functions of their position.

Coach educator: An individual that is specifically hired to design and evaluate educational programs and facilitate learning experiences to a specific group of coaches.[9] In youth sport, a coach educator typically operates outside the youth sport organization within a coaching association, national governing body of sport, national sport organization, or a higher education institution. The coach educator can also serve as a coach developer.

Interscholastic/scholastic coach: A middle school or high school coach working in a school-sponsored sport program.

Parent/guardian: The youth sport athlete's biological parents or legal guardians.

Peers: A friend, group of friends, teammates, or extended family members of the youth sport athlete that influence his or her experience in sport.

Private sport coach: An individual serving as the owner/operator or hired by a private business to provide fundamental skill development training in a specific sport or across multiple sports for youth sport athletes.

Sport administrator: An individual that oversees the management and operations of a youth sport program. In youth sport, the sport administrator may have additional duties within the organization or school district not related to the oversight of the youth program. The sport administrator often serves as a coach developer and may even serve as a coach educator.

Volunteer coach: An individual that offers his or her time and skills for no compensation. In youth sport, a volunteer coach is often a parent or a guardian but can also be a high school or college student or a member of the community.

Youth sport athlete: An individual between the ages of 6 and 18 that enrolls in participation- or performance-based sport in one or more of the following settings: community programs, club sport, scholastic sport, or private sport entities.

THE PATH TO BECOMING A YOUTH SPORT COACH

A youth sport coach is a person who creates a quality sport experience and guides the physical, psychological, and social-emotional development of youth athletes on their team.[10] The path to becoming a youth sport coach differs considerably. For example, parents, with varying degrees of experience, have been asked to coach their child's sport team. Other times, teachers, with varying degrees of experience, have been encouraged to coach a high school team. Also, trained coaches have applied for and accepted positions in a club, school, or community-based sport program. Regardless of the path, many parents, teachers, coaches, administrators, and community leaders are recognizing the importance of having some level of education and guidelines in order to provide youth athletes a quality sport experience. Further, professional organizations for coaches (e.g., SHAPE America) and coach educators/developers (e.g., United Center for Coaching Excellence) have outlined requirements for sport coaching.

SHAPE (Society of Health and Physical Educators) America[11] recommends that all youth sport coaches meet the following requirements prior to coaching:

- Submit to a background check
- Participate in an organization orientation that includes review of the coaches code of conduct
- Attain CPR and first aid certification
- Complete a basic coach education course aligned with the National Standards for Sport Coaches, preferably from an accredited program
- Seek opportunities for further professional development.

Currently, these requirements vary from organization to organization. However, many national organizations have introduced requirements and recommendations for coaching. While it is not possible to highlight all of these organizations, we provide insight into three.

1. The National Alliance for Youth Sports[12] requires all youth sport coach members to complete a coaching training program and sign their code of ethics. Upon becoming a member, they receive additional coaching resources and continuing education opportunities.
2. Many national governing bodies in the Olympic and Paralympic movement also have requirements for coaching in their system. For example, to obtain a coach membership with USA Swimming[13] coaches need to complete courses in foundation of coaching, rules and regulation, safety training (e.g., concussion training and water safety training for swim coaches), athlete protection training, and antidoping training. Additionally, coaches must attain CPR and first aid certification and submit to a background check. Once a member, additional coaching resources (e.g., journals) and professional development opportunities are provided.
3. Most state high school associations provide recommendations and requirements for coaching at the scholastic level. While these requirements vary from state to state, many programs require coaches to be teachers within the school (i.e., have an undergraduate degree and teacher licensure), submit to a background check, and complete coach education training that

includes safety training (e.g., first aid, concussion, child abuse recognition and prevention). Some state associations also offer professional development opportunities in conjunction with state coaches associations.

WHAT THE YOUTH COACH NEEDS TO KNOW AND DO

After reviewing the previous section, coaches may wonder what specifically they should be able to know and do to meet the demands and duties of a youth sport coach. There are many resources that provide answers to this question. First, the National Standards for Sport Coaches[14] outlines the core coaching responsibilities for coaches. These duties include the following:

- Set vision, goals, and standards for sport program
- Engage in and support ethical practices
- Build relationships
- Develop a safe sport environment
- Create a positive and inclusive sport environment
- Conduct practices and prepare for competition
- Strive for continuous improvement.

Within each of these core responsibilities, coaches can find standards that outline specific knowledge and skill competencies that they can work toward achieving. Second, the Quality Coaching Framework[15] offers coaches guidance on the essential professional, interpersonal, and intrapersonal knowledge for coaches to acquire while focusing on athlete development and coach well-being. With this knowledge, youth sport coaches can seek out learning opportunities associated with these competencies. For example, looking for quality online courses and resources related to knowledge and skills, completing an undergraduate program or series of courses aligned with the National Standards for Sport Coaches, or finding books, like this one, to guide coaches in their journey. Whatever method that is chosen, it is important to recognize that becoming a better coach is a lifelong pursuit and it is important to find programs, resources, and mentors to help along the way.

HOW TO USE THIS BOOK

This book will speak directly to the coach or coach developer (sport administrator or coach educator) working in community youth sport programs, club sports, interscholastic sport, or private youth sport entities. However, in order to provide best practices across all youth sport settings, the book is written to reach coaches committed to serving and further developing as a coach. Thus, while a parent-volunteer coach can glean concepts within each section, all chapters go into more depth to appeal to an interscholastic coach. Within each chapter, current research in coaching, coach education, and coach development, in conjunction with hands-on experience, is used to offer practical suggestions to improve coaching practice in the youth sport setting.

Each chapter in the book stands on its own and includes real-world scenarios with practicing coaches in both performance and participation contexts. Coaches will be able to relate the "in action" examples to daily coaching practice, and those engaged in coach development will be able to apply practical strategies for the development and evaluation of their coaching staff. Each chapter offers both the coach and coach developer tips to guide application of the concepts presented in the chapter.

The book is organized into twelve chapters. Following this introductory chapter, chapter 1 examines the common reasons why people coach and includes techniques in self-reflection to help coaches discover their purpose as a coach. Chapter 2 explains how to establish standards and set a vision for a team or program. Chapter 3 uses ethical scenarios to emphasize the importance of the coach as a role model. Chapter 4 focuses on how to connect with others, develop interpersonal skills, and be intentional about building positive relationships. In chapter 5, coaches learn ways to create a positive climate that reinforces an inclusive environment for all athletes to develop. Chapter 6 offers coaches an approach to provide a safe environment for sport participation in their program. In chapter 7, coaches will examine the key areas to focus on in their role as a coach, including skill progression, training programs, competitive strategies, mental training, and life skills. Chapter 8 examines how coaches can implement the best methods and teaching strategies to reach their athletes. In chapter 9, coaches learn how to evaluate athlete performance using a variety of assessment methods, and in chapter 10 they learn how to make adjustments to improve strategic decision making. In the last chapter, chapter 11, coaches explore strategies to continue learning as a coach.

To Coach Is to Know Your Why

When youth participate in sport they have the opportunity to develop their physical, psychological, and social competencies.[1] However, just participating in sport will not guarantee this holistic development. One of the key factors in helping kids develop in sport and learn to enjoy being physically active is the coach. Coaches can set the stage by doing the following:

- making quality practice plans that develop technical and tactical skills and physical conditioning,
- establishing a sport climate that emphasizes enjoyment, camaraderie, and striving to reach potential, and
- intentionally creating opportunities for youth to build important life skills through sport participation.

Further, coaches play an important role in the life of young people by being a mentor, role model, educator, consultant, motivator, and so forth. However, becoming this type of coach does not just happen when one steps out onto the field. Developing quality coaching practices requires personal reflection, exposure to a variety of learning experiences, and practical application. In fact, when youth participate in sport with trained coaches, they are more likely to have better player outcomes (e.g., self-esteem, enjoyment, reduced anxiety), motivation, and life-skill development.[2,3] Therefore, it is important that coaches are prepared to coach, continue to develop as coaches, and understand why they are coaching. Coaching is an ongoing developmental journey. The journey begins with personal reflection to better understand the reasons why people coach and how coaches can reflect upon and develop their own *why*.

WHY DO PEOPLE COACH?

There are a variety of reasons why people become a sport coach. These reasons can be driven by external or internal motives. Some external motives may be that a person has a child who plays on the team and the team needs a coach. Parents do not want their child to have a bad coach so they volunteer to coach. Another motive might be a person's commitment to growing a sport in their area, therefore, they sign up to coach. Growing a sport may be driven by an external motive, such as personal income or developing a feeder program for a high school team. However, growing a sport can also be driven by internal motives; for example, people who want to give back to their community through volunteering as a sport coach, people who want to teach youth important skills through sport, or people who enjoy working with kids. When researchers investigate why individuals pursue coaching, they find support for internal motives for coaching. These motives include sharing their passion for and knowledge of the sport with others, supporting sport-specific and personal growth of athletes, creating a fun and positive team learning environment for athletes, encouraging discipline and respect, and having the opportunity to experience success and winning.[4,5] While it is helpful to understand why people choose to coach, it is important for coaches to consider their own why for coaching.

IN ACTION

WHY I COACH

Between playing and now coaching, I've spent more time with a basketball in my hand than anything else in my life. Basketball is my love. Coaching is my passion. As a young athlete I fell in love with basketball; the hard work, the struggles, the victories and most of all being a part of something bigger than myself. Now as a coach, basketball fills my soul even more than when I was playing. My greatest joy stems from the bonds I build with my players, many of which are still strong today. I coach because I believe in teaching the game of basketball and helping young players use the game to navigate and learn life lessons. I strive to inspire each athlete to learn to prepare and fight for what they want to achieve and to never give up until they get it. Coaching also helps me grow personally, by constantly challenging me to self-reflect and seek opportunities to learn from others. The intense nature of the sport itself ignites my competitive drive and channels my strategic thinking to scout, prepare, and develop a master plan to best develop my athletes and unite them as a team.

—Charlene Murphy, head girls' basketball
coach, the Branson School (CA)

WHAT IS IMPORTANT TO ME?

Before coaches address the question, "Why I coach?" they need to reflect on what is personally important. The following self-reflection exercise is a value-based approach to discovering what is important. The basis of this technique centers on identifying values, what they mean, and how they drive decisions. Coaches can use the following steps to reflect on what is important to them. An analysis of a coach applying the self-reflective exercise is provided in the scenario about Lauren the swimming coach later in this chapter.

Self-Reflection Exercise

Step 1: Make a List of Values

What do I value? What do I give worth to? Where do I spend my time and money? A value can be (a) a material item, such as a sports car or a motorcycle; (b) a form of leisure, like jogging, bird watching, or painting; (c) characteristics viewed as a path to success in society, such as hard work, commitment, and loyalty; (d) characteristics that have moral implications in regard to our relationships with others, such as respect, responsibility, or honesty; and (e) important people in our lives, for example, parents, teachers, coaches, and friends.

Step 2: Describe What Each Value Means
   The next step is to write a brief descriptive statement that depicts what each value on the list means. For example, if I value commitment, my description might read, "Dedication and focus to fulfill all my obligations and to model this approach for others."

Step 3: Prioritize the Value List
   Examine the list of values and descriptive statements and rank the values, with one being the most important value. Each value must be ranked, no ties. Test the value list. Think back to a scenario in which two values on the list were in conflict. Did one value override the other value when making a decision? While each value on the list is important, the ranking provides perspective on how values might come into conflict with each other and which are more important than others.

Step 4: Write a Personal Mission Statement
   A personal mission statement is a short description of the outcomes one wants to achieve. Use the value list with descriptive statements to draft a personal mission statement. The personal mission statement can be one word or one paragraph. The number of words does not matter as long as it provides guidance. An example of a personal mission statement might read, "To demonstrate respect toward others and to model my commitment to doing my best work and doing it on time." By reflecting on values and developing a personal mission statement, coaches provide a foundation for developing a coaching philosophy to guide coaching practice. But, there is one more important step: understanding why they are coaching.

DISCOVERING THE WHY
When coaches understand their why for coaching they discover their purpose as a coach and it provides the foundation for how they will coach. The why is built on what is important (i.e., values) in conjunction with internal and external motives for coaching noted earlier in this chapter. In addition, Joe Ehrmann, author of *InSideOut Coaching* and founder of the *InSideOut Initiative*, states that understanding your why involves coaches reflecting upon some additional questions, namely:[6]

- Why do I coach?
- Why do I coach the way I do?

- What does it feel like to be coached by me?
- How do I define success?

In using these questions and discovering his why, Coach Ehrmann was able to put the reason for why he was a coach into words. He stated, "I coach to help boys become men of empathy and integrity who will lead, be responsible, and change the world for good."[7] With an understanding of his why, he could be more intentional in his coaching practice. This influenced what lessons he focused on with players, what core values he made a part of his program, and how he interacted with his players. That is, his why (purpose) drove what he did in practice and how he did it. Martin Camiré and his colleagues[8] provide additional questions for youth sport coaches to consider as they reflect upon their purpose:

- Am I teaching what I want my athletes to learn through sport?
- Are my athletes having positive experiences in sport?
- Am I appropriately balancing winning with athlete development?

The answer to these questions will help the coach be clear about the life lessons and type of experience they want their athletes to have under their guidance.

Once a coach identifies their purpose it points them in a philosophical direction, providing them with a vision for how they will lead their athletes. This is often referred to as the coaching philosophy, which is demonstrated by the coaching style or the characteristics and actions displayed as a coach. Figure 1.1 demonstrates how personal values and a coach's purpose provides a vision to guide their actions as a coach in leading their team.

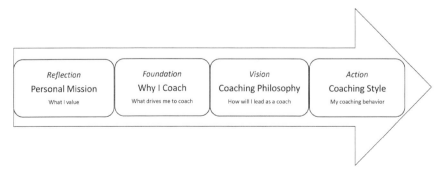

FIGURE 1.1
How Your *Why* Guides Coaching Action

HELPING COACHES KNOW THEIR WHY

As a coach goes through the hiring process, it can be difficult to discover if the coach is truly clear in their purpose. The best way to determine their clarity is to ask them directly. With program values and principles clearly established and integrated into the decision-making process, I assess the authenticity of a prospective coach through structured interviews. Experience and behavior-based questions help uncover the foundational values of a coach. The successful coach understands the sport through the eyes of the players. It has become clear to me over the years that if the coach is unable to explain their purpose for coaching in simple, repeatable terms, they do not truly understand it. If a coach speaks in more complicated verbose language, I follow up and ask them to explain it to me as if I were a new incoming athlete on their team. Good coaches adjust and handle this follow-up well. The truly great coaches never needed the follow-up. They knew their purpose and how to bring it to life.

In helping coaches reflect on their purpose for coaching, I have found that the power of listening speaks louder than any words I can use. Asking questions and getting feedback is critical to understanding their philosophy. What coaches do follows what they think. I have found that when coaches use goals to align where they want to go with what they need to get there, transformative things happen. To seek and understand the perspectives of coaches is essential to helping them develop their coaching philosophy and live it out daily. This also helps foster a dynamic environment of continuous professional learning within the program to sustain growth. More important, athletic administrators must also embrace and model the behaviors they wish to see in others. My mission in education is to help each person reveal and realize their full potential by empowering them to live a life of purpose with authenticity, empathy, and gratitude. My goal is not to help people be better, my goal is to help people be their best. Listening to coaches and helping them reflect on their purpose and align it with their goals is a foundational step in this process. When you know your why, you know your way.

—Rick Lilly, former director of student activities at Highland
Springs High School and current assistant principal
Highland Springs, VA

MY COACHING PHILOSOPHY

The process of developing a coaching philosophy involves the coach engaging in self-reflection and self-aware activities to determine important values, motivation for coaching, and purpose in coaching (e.g., outcomes sought for athletes). Once the coach has done this, the next step is to develop a coaching philosophy statement that aligns with their personal mission statement and their purpose for coaching. The coaching philosophy statement describes the manner in which the coach is going to lead their team and impact their athletes.[9] Coach Ehrmann's statement on why he coaches does this.

Another example of a coaching philosophy statement based on the personal mission statement listed in step four might read, "I will make a commitment to treating all athletes with respect and have a sincere interest in helping them learn and develop physical, psychological, social, and mental skills for long-term enjoyment in sport." There are multiple ways to draft a coaching philosophy statement. But, if a coach has engaged in self-reflection and is self-aware, their coaching philosophy statement should provide them guidance as a coach (see figure 1.1).

DOES MY WHY AND COACHING PHILOSOPHY MATCH MY COACHING CONTEXT?

Once a coaching philosophy is set it is also important for coaches to consider whether it fits their coaching context. A question coaches might ask is this: Can I enact my philosophy with my athletes at this level and in this sport? Taking time to evaluate whether the setting aligns with the coaching philosophy can help coaches determine the best environment in which to fulfill their purpose as a coach. Read the following scenario, respond to the three questions, and review the analysis to examine the importance of assessing how a coaching philosophy should align within a particular youth sport setting.

Scenario

Lauren has been a swimming coach for 12 years at the youth club level. She started coaching because she wanted to stay involved in the sport she was so passionate about while growing up. (Value swimming.)

Her approach to coaching is to share her passion for swimming, so that her athletes learn to enjoy the sport as much as she has. (Why I coach.)

Lauren believes that to enjoy the sport you need to learn how to swim well to compete at the top level. (Value competition.)

Thus, when asked about her coaching philosophy Lauren states that she seeks to share a passion for competitive swimming by creating a positive yet challenging training environment for swimmers to develop their swimming performance. (Coaching philosophy.)

Lauren's coaching style could be described as intense. She likes to design drills and training programs that challenge her athletes to go beyond their "comfort zone," so that they learn what they are capable of. (Coaching behavior demanding.)

While she pushes her athletes hard, she is extremely positive in her approach and is good at building their confidence and making it an enjoyable experience. (Coaching behavior positive attitude.)

Lauren recently moved to a new community and is looking for opportunities to coach swimming. She notices a job announcement for a swim instructor/coach at a local summer camp for youth, 9–12 years old. The summer camp will run for eight weeks and the position is to provide basic swim instruction, conduct swimming activities/games, and supervise free swim time. Lauren is interested in the position and meets all of the job qualifications.

Questions

1. What is it about Lauren's coaching philosophy and/or coaching style that does not match the youth camp position?
2. Is it possible that Lauren could adapt her coaching style to meet the needs of this position? Why or why not?
3. Should Lauren take the job or should the athletic administrator hire her for this position?

Analysis

Based on the information provided in the scenario, we might consider Lauren's coaching philosophy to align with her why for coaching. Lauren has a passion for swimming and she strives to help athletes enjoy the sport while preparing them for competitive success in the pool. This approach drives her coaching style, which is demanding, but positive. Although Lauren's coaching philosophy does appear to include a focus on skill development (question 1), which aligns with the goals of the youth camp to develop swimming skills, she may struggle to adapt to the noncompetitive environment of the camp.

When considering this swim instructor/coach position (question 2), Lauren will be better equipped to make the right decision if she is clear on what her purpose is as a coach. By operating with a coaching philosophy built on her values, Lauren can evaluate if the position is a good fit. In this scenario, she would recognize that the supervision of free swim time and organizing swimming games may not fulfill her competitive spirit (i.e., personal value). However, by identifying how her coaching philosophy does not align with the position, she can choose to adapt her approach or no longer pursue the opportunity.

Since the youth camp position is temporary and the sport organization hosting the camp hires a large number of coaches, the interview process is likely not extensive. In addition, Lauren has already proven herself as a swimming coach and she meets all the qualifications on the job description (question 3). Therefore, it might be easier for the program director to accept her credentials as a coach and hire her for the position. However, to guarantee Lauren is a good fit, the director will want to ask her some additional questions to confirm she understands the expectations of the position, for example,

- How do you think your instructional style fits our summer camp program?
- How do you approach your role as a swim instructor?
- How will you organize swimming games that focus on participation?

CONCLUSION

While there are a variety of reasons why people coach youth sport, when coaches understand the reason why they are coaching they are better prepared to lead youth in a manner that matches the setting they work in and their coaching philosophy.

COACH TIPS!

- Reflect on what is important and draft a list of values, describing what they mean.
- Write a personal mission statement to clarify beliefs and values.
- Seek to understand the internal and external motives for coaching.
- Write a coaching philosophy statement that aligns with the personal mission statement and the why.

- Before taking a coaching position, reflect on coaching philosophy and make sure it aligns with the organization so as to prepare to adapt or decide not to take the position.

COACH DEVELOPER TIPS!

- Assist coaches in reflective practice to establish a personal mission and coaching philosophy.
- Implement postseason reflection activities with coaches to help them monitor and evaluate their continued alignment with their coaching philosophy.
- Evaluate if the coaches hired to work with youth have a coaching philosophy that matches the coaching context they will be working in.

2

To Coach Is to Know Your Role

In leading youth athletes, the role of the coach is to provide instruction and guidance for individual and team development. To accomplish this, coaches establish a vision based on their core values and coaching philosophy and set standards of performance based on long-term athlete development. Thus, coaching practice is guided by a vision based on core values, coaching philosophy, and standards of performance. To demonstrate how coaching philosophy guides practice and helps plan for athlete development, consider the following case of Coach Thompson.

THE CASE OF COACH THOMPSON

Tony Thompson shuffled toward a group of youth lacrosse players. His eyes shifted downward as he walked, focused on the practice plan he held in his left hand. Today was the first practice of the season. As he neared the group, Coach Thompson could sense their energy. It was the same energy he felt at the beginning of each lacrosse club sport season. This would be Coach Thompson's fourth season coaching the U14 team. The U14 team was one of several teams under the Canyon River Lacrosse Club System. A nonprofit, parent-run organization, Canyon River Lacrosse provides skill development and competition for youth ages 9–18 through summer camps, training programs, and competitive teams. The organization has been in operation for 10 years and Tony is one of eight coaches in the program.

A former collegiate athlete in football and track at a small four-year liberal arts college, Tony married his college sweetheart and they decided to move back to Tony's hometown to start a family. Tony would work for the family's insurance agency and his wife would build her career as a financial advisor. The Thompsons had two children. Both were heavily involved in youth sports including soccer, basketball, and volleyball. But, one afternoon, their oldest daughter was invited by a friend to a free skills clinic held by Canyon River Lacrosse. After the clinic, she was hooked and wanted to sign up. Tony had already been involved in coaching youth soccer for five years but had never played lacrosse or much less watched a match. Nonetheless, to stay involved in his daughter's youth sport experience, Tony asked the U12 lacrosse coach if he could serve as her assistant to help her run practice sessions and learn the game. Canyon River Lacrosse did not offer training for their coaches, but they did require a background check.

The Thompsons quickly noticed how their daughter took to lacrosse and the positive experience she was having with the U12 team. After two years serving as an apprentice under his daughter's U12 coach, there was an opening for the U14 coaching position. Tony felt ready for this opportunity, and he had really grown to love the sport. He also saw it as an opportunity to keep coaching his daughter. He approached the club about serving as the coach and was offered the position.

Over the next few years, Coach Thompson shared his passion for lacrosse by creating a positive culture for his athletes to learn and experience the game. He also developed a good rapport with the parents, and his reputation in the lacrosse community was of a coach that made the game fun. However, Coach Thompson began to recognize where he lacked specific training as a coach and started to question his qualifications as a lacrosse coach. He knew he needed to become a better coach in his ability to teach the technical and tactical skills of the sport. This, in turn, had an impact on his confidence and effectiveness as a coach. In addition, his experience as an athlete with mental and physical skill training was outdated, and he had no formal training to provide him with a new foundation to teach each skill appropriately to the U14 girls' team. Although the U14 team was always competitive, each season Coach Thompson's teams had about the same number of wins and losses.

As Tony stood before his new team, about to begin a new season, he felt a sense of confidence. This season was going to be his best yet as a coach.

At the end of the previous season, he felt he could do more as a coach and even though he was respected as a coach in the Canyon River Lacrosse Club, he wanted to win more games. Thus, he became a student of the game. He learned how to teach the game better, how to be a stronger leader, and how to challenge young athletes to meet a higher standard. But more important, he took time to reflect on his personal values and why he was coaching. This allowed him to develop a coaching philosophy statement as well as create standards of performance to help guide his coaching action. Now, in this moment, as he stood before his team, he had the opportunity to apply what he had learned.

Review and Reflection

The first two chapters reviewed the pathway to becoming a coach and developing a coaching philosophy by helping coaches understand their values and purpose associated with coaching. To review this content, consider the following questions:

1. Based on the information provided, how would you describe why Tony is coaching?
2. Although Tony was able to recognize some areas he needs to improve on as a coach, what other areas do you think he might be lacking or may need additional training?
3. What is the Canyon River Lacrosse Club's role in educating their coaches? Do you feel they were meeting this responsibility? Why or why not?

Coach Thompson's Offseason Reflection

Recognizing his limitations, Tony embarked on an offseason improvement plan. As he reflected on what is important to him, he was able to develop a list of personal values, a personal mission statement, and a coaching philosophy statement, which are outlined below.

Coach Thompson's Prioritized Personal Value List with Action Statements

1. Family: My immediate and extended family comes first in any and all decisions that may potentially impact them.
2. Health: I make time to engage in regular exercise and strive to make healthy eating choices for long-term health.

3. Faith: I make time to practice regular prayer and worship for my spiritual health and well-being.

4. Respect: I can learn from each and every person I meet regardless of their beliefs or social status and strive to treat every person with dignity.

5. Responsibility: I strive to help others by being accountable for my actions and by holding others to the same standard.

6. Trust: I strive to act with integrity in all interactions with others to develop healthy long-term relationships.

7. Knowledge: I engage in ongoing learning activities to stay current on topics related to my business and my role as the coach of the U14 girls' lacrosse team.

Coach Thompson's Personal Mission Statement

I will demonstrate respect and responsibility in my interactions with others to build positive relationships, while staying true to my family, health, and faith.

Coach Thompson's Coaching Philosophy Statement

I coach to share my passion for lacrosse. I will connect with my athletes to teach them the skills of playing the game, how to be respectful toward others and honor the game. I will build trust within my team by treating all athletes with respect and fulfill my responsibilities as a role model by being a knowledgeable and relatable coach.

Building on this reflective exercise, Coach Thompson was ready to take the next step and establish standards of performance for this team. But, first he needed to align with the core values of the Canyon River Lacrosse Club.

CORE VALUES TO GUIDE COACHING PRACTICE

In 2004, the USA Basketball team brought home a bronze medal from the Olympics in Athens, Greece. By all accounts, this was a low point for USA Basketball. Since the famed Dream Team in 1992, composed of professional athletes, international competition had been catching up to the United States in the sport of basketball. For those involved in USA Basketball, something had to change. A committee composed of some of the most respected names in US basketball at that time convened in 2005 and courted Duke University men's basketball coach Mike Krzyzewski to lead Team USA.[1] Coach Krzyzewski (Coach K) was already a hall of fame basketball coach and well respected for his ability to teach the game and motivate his athletes. In addition, he was an accomplished coach on the scoreboard. In 2005, Coach K had already won three NCAA Division I National Championships in 1991, 1992, and 2001.[2] He was an easy pick by the committee and he accepted. Therefore, in 2005, Coach K would begin an 11-year run (2005–2016) as the head coach of the Men's National Team. In 2008, Coach K in collaboration with members of the 2008 USA Men's Basketball National Team created the Team USA Gold Standards. The 15 Gold Standards set expectations to guide behavior for the national team's quest for a gold medal. For example, one of the standards was no excuses, which was described as "We have what it takes to win." Another example was communication, listed as "We look each other in the eye and we tell each other the truth."[3]

Today, the Gold Standards permeate all aspects of USA Basketball from the national team through their junior national team program. They serve as guidance in the development of individual athletes by communicating the expectations for every member of the team. Furthermore, the Gold Standards hold each athlete accountable to one another and provide common ground for all coaches and athletes working under the USA Basketball umbrella in guiding behavior.

The Gold Standards established by Coach K and the Olympic athletes could also be described as core values. Core values are the guiding beliefs about how an organization or group is going to act and interact with one another.[4] Core values guide behavior, setting a standard to which individuals must adhere to for the organization or group to be successful in achieving their goals. For Coach K and the national team, the Gold Standards were shared core values which each member of the team made a commitment.

Establishing core values can occur at the organizational level (e.g., USA Basketball) or within an individual program. For example, the Canyon River Lacrosse Club could have the following core values:

Canyon River Lacrosse Core Values

Performance
- We work each day to improve our individual skills.

Competitiveness
- We always give our best effort.
- We prepare for each opponent by paying attention to detail.
- We execute the game plan during each match.

Resilience
- We turn a negative setback on the field of play into a positive.
- We move on to the "next play."
- We increase our work ethic to improve individual performance following a setback.

Pride
- We exhibit confidence on and off the field of play.
- We work hard each day to improve individually and as a team.
- We are humble in our success and gracious in losses.

Friendship
- We are welcoming to everyone on the team.
- We support each other.
- We celebrate the success of all members of our team.

Responsibility
- We will be on time.
- We are accountable for actions on and off the field of play.
- We fulfill our role on the team.

Teamwork
- We share in our success and failure together.
- We encourage and support a positive environment within our team.
- We follow the game plan and share the ball.

Integrity
- We tell the truth when communicating with others.
- We honor the game by following the rules of play.
- We are respectful to each other and opposing teams.

When the core values are organization driven, then a coach working in the organization needs to align their coaching philosophy with the expectations of the organization. However, if the organization does not have established core values, the coach can develop core values for their team that align directly with their coaching philosophy.

IN ACTION

CORE VALUES TO GUIDE PROGRAM DEVELOPMENT

At USA Basketball, we center all of our youth programs around three core standards: fun, safety, and development. We service a diverse audience and understand that audience is critical to program development. A great program is one which fulfills a need in the community. Making basketball fun improves the likelihood a child will stay involved in the sport, especially at early levels. Our safety measures ensure coaches working with youth are properly screened and trained. Proper development stems from a progressive basketball curriculum that teaches players skills based on their individual ability levels. These core standards allow us to provide positive experiences to grow the game nationwide. We reinforce our core program standards by performing yearly assessments to evaluate our processes and outcomes against these goals. By surveying and communicating with our audience, we determine our effectiveness in these areas. As an organization, we have to be willing to reorganize or abolish a program if we can't find a way for it to promote our standards. If not, we are sending the message that these things aren't truly important to us. By incorporating fun, safety, and development into every program we offer, we convey the message that basketball is for everyone and the player experience matters.

—Andrea Travelstead, assistant director,
youth & sport development, USA Basketball

ESTABLISHING STANDARDS FOR ATHLETE DEVELOPMENT

Once the coach has either aligned or established core values to guide the behavior of athletes and coaches within their program/team, the coach can set measurable expectations or standards of performance (SoP) to guide and assess individual and/or team performance. The evaluation of athlete performance can be ongoing throughout the season, be assessed at the end of the season, or a combination of both. In developing SoP, the youth sport administrator and/or youth coach would identify the needs of the athlete and then create specific outcomes which would guide coaches in teaching their athletes. While coaches and administrators may have some ideas about the specific athlete outcomes they would like to achieve, understanding athlete development might be a helpful guide for creating comprehensive SoP.

Athlete development involves coaches considering how they can engage in coaching practices that will promote the physical, psychological, and social-emotional development of their athletes. One way to conceptualize this development is to use the 4 C's of athlete development. The 4 C's originated from decades of research and review on best coaching practices and how to be an effective coach.[5] This framework outlines the following four areas of athlete outcomes: competence, confidence, connection, and character.

- Competence includes aspects of physical development that make it possible for youth to participate in a wide variety of physical activities. These aspects of physical development include developing fundamental movement patterns (e.g., running or jumping), learning the technical and tactical skills associated with a sport, and building physical fitness (e.g., endurance, speed, strength).
- Confidence is the belief in one's ability to perform in a sport setting.[6] Developing this confidence not only requires physical competence but also psychological skills. These psychological skills include setting goals, using constructive self-talk, imagining positive images, managing stress, and focusing. By working on these skills, athletes build their mental strengths, which support a more realistic belief in their capabilities and assist them when they face adversity.
- Connection entails the ability to connect with and work well with others. To do this successfully requires a set of social-emotional skills. These skills include: learn to control one's emotions, treat others with respect and kindness, understand another person's thoughts and feelings (i.e., empathy), collaborate with others, communicate effectively, and resolve conflicts.
- Character involves helping youth act in ways that positively contribute to their sport teams and their communities. To contribute positively on sport teams, athletes learn the importance of ethical play (e.g., being a good sport, playing fair, helping others) and life skills (e.g., being a leader, being a team player, being accountable, making good decisions). It is hoped that

the skills are then transferred to other life contexts; for example, helping neighbors during a crisis, being a positive role model in school, and being responsible at home.

While there is not one method that must be followed when developing standards of performance, using the 4 C's provides a holistic approach in creating SoP for each coaching context. Table 2.1 provides some guiding questions for coaches to consider in developing SoP using the 4 C's of athlete development. The examples pertain to Coach Thompson's U14 team.

Table 2.1. Developing Standards of Performance Using 4 C's

Questions for Holistic Development	Sample SoPs for Coach Thompson
Competence	
• What technical, tactical, and performance skills do youth need to be able to demonstrate at the end of this program or season? • What level of physical conditioning do athletes need to have in terms of endurance, strength, speed, and flexibility? • How may this differ by athletes' age, growth, and maturation?	• Athletes improve agility/footwork by decreasing their time on the zig-zag cone drill by 20 percent. • Athletes improve their endurance during the season by running 20 percent on their one-mile run. • Athletes exhibit mastery of offensive skills in competitive situations (e.g., improving successful passes during a game).
Confidence	
• How will I evaluate whether the youth under my guidance demonstrated confidence and resilience? • What mental skills do athletes need to develop or master during the season?	• Athletes show resiliency by reducing the number of repeat errors in games by 20 percent. • All athletes show confident body language at the start of the game by the end of the season. • 80 percent of athletes make progress on their end-of-season goals.
Connection	
• What interpersonal skills do youth need to demonstrate by the end of the program and/or season?	• Athletes increase on the field communication by 25 percent by the end of the season. • Athletes demonstrate conflict resolution skills to resolve minor disputes on the team without coach intervention at least once during the season. • Captains devise at least three team-building activities for the team during the season.

(continued)

Table 2.1. *Continued*

Questions for Holistic Development	Sample SoPs for Coach Thompson
Character	
• How will I evaluate whether youth under my guidance engage in fair play, respect for the sport, and be a good sport? • What life skills (e.g., responsibility, decision making) do I need athletes to demonstrate aligned with program purpose and are appropriate for their age?	• Athletes always shake hands with opponents after games and maintain self-control even after losing. • By the middle of the season, athletes take more ownership of their training by leading warm-ups and cool-down.

STANDARDS TO GUIDE COACHING PRACTICE

At Vandal Aquatic Club, we believe the art of coaching athletes is based on four core values: respect, responsibility, service above self, and excellence in everything. As head age group coach, my role is to present these values in simple and effective ways so that they are understood, accepted, and integrated into the personal actions of the athletes and coaches on a daily basis. We are able to do this, even with young athletes, by focusing on real-life behaviors.

Respect can be as simple as one person speaks at a time and when your coach speaks, everyone listens. Responsibility can be demonstrated by being prepared for practice, such as bringing a full water bottle and extra swim goggles. Service above self centers on being kind and valuing the thoughts and experiences of others, especially when they are different from our own. Excellence in everything focuses on process-based learning: Have I done my best today to do my best today? We encourage our athletes to see their sport and their life through this lens. Most important, do my athletes and fellow coaches see these values in me? Am I demonstrating respect for them and their efforts through my words and actions? Have I arrived at practice with a plan, my stopwatches, and my water bottle? Do I keep up on current best practices in my sport? Do I care about who they are as a person at the pool and away from the pool? My role as head age group coach is an honor and a privilege, and I strive to express these core values in everything I do, both on the deck and off.

—Jody Rash, head age group coach, Vandal Aquatic Club (Moscow, ID)

PLANNING FOR COACHING PRACTICE

In 38 seasons at the University of Tennessee as the head women's basketball coach, Pat Summitt won eight NCAA Division I National Championships and more than 1,000 games.[7] The manner in which Coach Summitt led her collegiate basketball program was driven by a coaching philosophy that reflected her purpose as a coach. In other words, Coach Summitt had a clear vision for how she would conduct herself as a coach and how she would lead her basketball program. Coach Summitt knew her why as a coach (i.e., purpose) and had an established coaching philosophy (i.e., personal values to guide coaching practice) that drove her coaching style (i.e., coaching behaviors). Coach Summitt also had established core values to communicate her expectations and to guide her plan for coaching the University of Tennessee basketball team. Her core values are captured in what she called the Definite Dozen. Coach Summitt's Definite Dozen[8] is listed below, the core value noted in parentheses has been added for emphasis.

1. Respect Yourself and Others (respect)
2. Take Full Responsibility (responsibility)
3. Develop and Demonstrate Loyalty (loyalty)
4. Learn to Be a Great Communicator (communication)
5. Discipline Yourself So No One Else Has To (discipline)
6. Make Hard Work Your Passion (hard work)
7. Don't Just Work Hard, Work Smart (preparation)
8. Put the Team before Yourself (teamwork)
9. Make Winning an Attitude (winning)
10. Be a Competitor (competition)
11. Change Is a Must (adaptable)
12. Handle Success like You Handle Failure (humility)

Coach Summitt shared her Definite Dozen with her athletes at the beginning and throughout the season.[9] Furthermore, the Definite Dozen served as standards of performance for each athlete and the team in regard to how they practiced, conditioned, and competed. For example, in Make Hard Work Your Passion, Coach Summitt set an expectation that all athletes and coaches in her basketball program would outwork everybody in college basketball.[10] Collegiate basketball athletes knew this before making a commitment to Coach Summitt's program, and once they were on campus this expectation was role modeled by veteran players and Coach Summitt through their daily habits, such as coming early to work, pushing through minor setbacks, and not accepting poor performance based on lack of effort.[11]

By operating with a clear purpose and coaching philosophy, youth coaches can plan for daily coaching practice that incorporate already established core values and SoP, either organization driven (e.g., USA Basketball) or coach designed (e.g., Coach Pat Summit or Coach Thompson's U14 team). Unlike the coaching philosophy, which provides consistent guidance for coaching practice over time, planning for coaching practice is adapted each season or at the start of a new training period to fit the needs of your team or group (see figure 2.1).

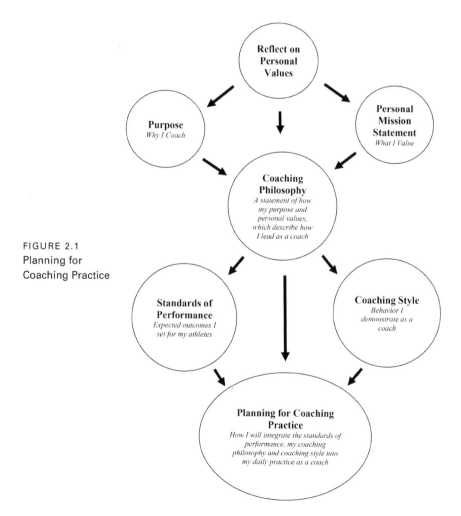

FIGURE 2.1
Planning for
Coaching Practice

Planning for coaching practice are the actions taken each day to meet the expectations outlined by the program's core values and SoP. Whereas SoPs establish expectations for athletes, planning for coaching practice is also part of the coach's action plan. In other words, a blueprint for (a) planning skill progression, training programs, competitive strategies, mental training, and life-skill development for their team (see chapter 7), and (b) teaching technical and tactical skills to improve the confidence and ability of their athletes (see chapter 8). While the plan for coaching practice may be similar each season, it should be adjusted to the current team being coached. For example, a veteran high school tennis coach has a team of underclassmen for the upcoming season. Knowing her team is young, she might need to adjust her plan for coaching practice to best meet the needs of this year's squad. Table 2.2 is a checklist that provides coaches an opportunity to reflect on their readiness to begin planning for coaching practice.

Table 2.2. Planning for Coaching Checklist

✓	Planning for Coaching Practice Checklist
☐	I have fulfilled the requirements for coaching by completing one or more of the following: • A background check • An organization established coach orientation program • A review of the coaches code of conduct • Acquiring appropriate safety certification • Completing a basic coach education course aligned with the National Standards for Sport Coaches (introduction)
☐	I have identified what is important to me by reflecting on my personal values (ch. 1)
☐	I have written a personal mission statement that reflects what I value (ch. 1)
☐	I have identified my purpose as a coach or why I am coaching (ch. 1)
☐	I have written a coaching philosophy statement built on my personal values and purpose as a coach (ch. 1)
☐	I have matched my coaching philosophy to my coaching context (ch. 1)
☐	I have established standards of performance for my program and/or team aligned with holistic athlete development or I am aligning my coaching practice with standards already established by the organization I coach under (ch. 2)

CONCLUSION

While the role of the coach can be complex, by staying focused on why they are coaching and planning for coaching practice, coaches will be able to improve on their coach effectiveness. Furthermore, by completing the steps outlined in the introduction and chapters 1–2, coaches have a template to guide them in planning for their upcoming season or program. Once a plan is established they can begin to create a climate for athlete growth and development.

COACH TIPS!

- Identify the core values for the program.
- Establish standards of performance for the program and/or team based on the development of athletes using the 4 C's (competence, confidence, connection, and character).
- Adapt your coaching plan each season to best meet the needs of athletes while staying true to coaching philosophy and purpose.

COACH DEVELOPER TIPS!

- Implement the 4 C's model to assist coaches in developing program standards.
- Encourage coaches to develop and reflect upon their core values or develop core values for the organization based on input from all coaches.
- Discuss with coaches the connection between their core values, coaching philosophy, and standards of performance.
- Evaluate the progress of a coach in providing a holistic athlete development experience.

3

To Coach Is to
Be a Role Model

It goes without saying that a coach should demonstrate ethical practice in leading athletes. In youth sport, administrators, parents, and the community expect that coaches will avoid behavior that is harmful to the physical, mental, and social development of each athlete, such as verbal or physical abuse and harassment; while at the same time promote fair play and role model good sportsmanship. Coaches, who respect each athlete and fulfill their responsibility to teach fair play and reinforce good sport conduct, are operating with an ethical mind-set. An ethical mind-set can be described as the motives and intentions that guide one's desire to act in an ethical manner. In other words, one's ethical mind-set is reflected in their character traits or specific qualities unique to them, such as loyalty and kindness. An ethical mind-set is also influenced by personal values (see chapter 1).

Developmental psychologist, educator, and author Thomas Lickona describes the development of one's character as the interaction between moral knowing, moral feeling, and moral action.[1] Moral knowing is understanding moral values and being able to implement perspective taking when making decisions. For example, a coach should know that the use of derogatory language toward an athlete could potentially harm an athlete emotionally. Therefore, by stating a degrading remark the coach would be demonstrating a lack of respect (moral value) toward the athlete and it may hurt them emotionally (perspective taking). Lickona referred to moral knowing as "knowing the good" or "habits of the mind."[2]

Moral feeling is built from our conscience, self-esteem, empathy, self-control, and humility. While the coach may know that the use of a degrading remark is inappropriate, does the coach have the desire to maintain self-control and be empathic toward the athlete? According to Lickona, this is the ability to "desire the good" or "habits of the heart."[3] If the coach "knows the good" (avoiding the use of degrading words) and "desires the good," the coach can take moral action or "do the good" and avoid the use of the degrading term. In other words, the coach has developed competence and the strength to operate in an ethical manner. Lickona describes taking moral action as the "habits of action."[4]

The development of an ethical mind-set is influenced by education, the environment, and moral role models (figure 3.1).[5] The educational setting challenges students to develop critical thinking skills. When there is a deliberate attempt to discuss ethical issues by the teacher, the student may develop stronger reasoning skills to deal with ethical scenarios. In conjunction with education, one's ethical mind-set is influenced by the varied environments in which they play, work, and learn. If the environment promotes or fails to promote *moral feeling* and *moral action*, then over time this will have an impact on one's ethical mind-set. The impact of education and varied environments will be positively or negatively influenced by moral role models operating in both settings, including parents, teachers, coaches, peers, and siblings.

Even with a solid educational background, the influence of strong moral role models, and being a part of positive environments in sport, youth sport coaches will be faced with making decisions that challenge the ethical mind-set they have established. In the following scenario, examine how Coach Lawson's decision is a reflection of his ethical mind-set.

ETHICAL SCENARIO 1: ACCIDENTAL EAVESDROPPING

Marty Lawson strode off the football field toward the locker room at a steady pace. Marty was only four years removed from his high school playing career and was serving his first season as an assistant high school football coach. Today was his day to supervise the locker room. As he entered the building and barreled down the stairs toward the team changing area, Marty's left knee twinged with pain from the three knee surgeries he endured over four years. The surgeries had prematurely ended his chances of a collegiate

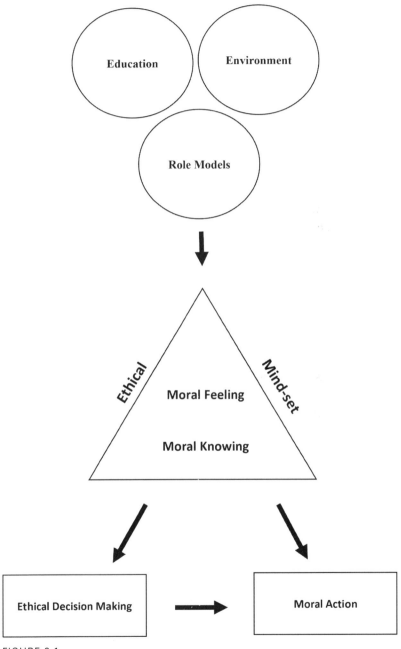

FIGURE 3.1
Ethical Mindset

football career, leading him to his current coaching role sooner than he expected. His pace slowed as he approached the locker room and he could hear several athletes boasting about a team initiation event this coming Friday. Then he heard a player say, "Shush, one of the coaches might be coming." Marty paused his stride briefly and then continued into the locker room. The athletes became eerily quiet for a locker room full of teenagers. Uncomfortable in the moment, Marty decided to diffuse the silence with a comment about an amazing catch made by one of the athletes during practice. The stillness passed and athletes began jabbering about the catch and boasting about their own prowess on the field. Marty distanced himself to the coach's office and waited for the other coaches. Alone with his thoughts, Marty contemplated what he should say about what he overheard. Although he had participated in a few initiation-type activities as a football player, he understood that this type of behavior was unacceptable and against school policy. Marty even recalled the athletic director discussing the dangers of not monitoring potential hazing-type activity during the preseason coaches meeting. Furthermore, he had been at the receiving end of a hazing incident and could still remember the humiliation. But he was conflicted. A little hazing seemed like a normal part of playing football, at least on the teams he played on and his coaches had never intervened. Plus, the athletes would probably know that he had heard them in the locker room and turned them in. Besides, he thought hesitantly, I turned out fine. As the other coaches piled into the coaches' office, Marty decided to just ignore what he had overheard.

COACH LAWSON'S ETHICAL MIND-SET

Coach Marty Lawson's ethical mind-set is on display in this scenario. Using Lickona's model, we can further examine the development of Coach Lawson's ethical mind-set.

- Moral knowing: Coach Lawson's inexperience as a coach and his age (mid-twenties), may limit his experience and understanding of moral values. Even though he is aware of the potential dangers of hazing-type behavior (education received during preseason coaches meetings), he may not understand the moral implications (lack of respect or harm). In addition, he may lack formal training (education) on how to recognize and deal with scenarios involving hazing.

- Moral feeling: Coach Lawson may be empathic toward athletes at the receiving end of a hazing initiation based on his previous experience. The conflict he is feeling hints that his conscience tells him this type of behavior is unacceptable. Yet, his lack of moral coaching role models during his athletic career in regard to hazing may limit his ability to demonstrate empathy in this scenario, as Marty may feel that hazing is a normal part of playing football.
- Moral action: Possibly due to his inexperience as a coach, lack of formal training as a coach, and previous experience as an athlete, where hazing-type behavior seemed to be accepted, Coach Lawson may lack the competence to take moral action and share his concern with the coaching staff.

ETHICAL DECISION MAKING

The ethical mind-set coupled with personal values of coaches guide their ability to make decisions that have ethical implications. In 2012, Joe Paterno passed away at the age of 85. Coach Paterno was a highly successful collegiate football coach for 46 years at Penn State University, where he amassed 409 wins and two national championships.[6] More importantly, he was viewed as a man of high integrity. Coach Paterno valued education, and he developed strong character values in the young men he coached. His loyalty to Penn State was evident in his commitment to staying at the university for 46 years, where he was an advocate for education, donating more than four million to the university.[7] Nevertheless, Coach Paterno's loyalty to Penn State was second to his commitment to the football program, where loyalty ran deep among former players and his coaching staff. Coach Paterno's ethical mind-set was built on strong personal values, his educational experience, and moral role models throughout his life. His ethical mind-set was also influenced by the culture (i.e., environment) he created over the years in his football program—a mind-set that would ultimately lead to removal as the head football coach at Penn State.

According to public record, Coach Paterno became aware of an assistant coach on his staff, Jerry Sandusky, acting inappropriately toward young boys.[8] What Coach Paterno knew and when he knew it rests with him. But, before his passing Coach Paterno stated he wishes he would have done more, a strong hint that he knew and regretted a decision he made in the past.[9] The decision Coach Paterno made or failed to make is an example of a moral action he took as a result of making a decision when faced with an ethical dilemma.

An ethical dilemma is "when you are placed in a situation where what you believe is challenged or questioned and you are forced to act."[10] Thus, ethical dilemmas occur when there is a conflict of moral and social character values. A moral character value has a direct impact on others and influences how we treat and interact with other people. An example of a moral character value is responsibility. I am accountable for my actions (i.e., how my behavior has an impact on others) and I have an obligation to care for others. A social value has an impact on how I achieve success as determined by society. An example of a social value is hard work. If I work hard, I have the chance to reach the goals I set for myself. The list below has some common moral and social character values. Coaches can revisit the personal values they listed in the self-reflection exercise from chapter 1 and identify which values are moral character values and which are social character values.

Common Social and Moral Character Values
- Social character values

  - Hard work
  - Winning
  - Toughness
  - Loyalty
  - Intensity
  - Commitment

- Moral character values

  - Integrity
  - Honesty
  - Respect
  - Responsibility
  - Beneficence
  - Justice

HOW AN ETHICAL MIND-SET LEADS TO ETHICAL DECISION MAKING

When coaches are faced with an ethical dilemma involving a conflict between moral and social character values, such as the situation Coach Paterno faced at Penn State, they will rely on their ethical mind-set, developed over time, to guide them in making ethical decisions. If we revisit the case of Coach Lawson, we can examine how his ethical mind-set guides him through the ethical decision-making process when dealing with conflicting values associated with an ethical dilemma.

Coach Lawson's Ethical Mind-set

Consistent behavior over time indicates the manner in which one approaches ethical scenarios. Because Coach Lawson is conflicted on the best course of action to take in regard to reporting the potential hazing incident or not (ethical dilemma), he demonstrates that he understands the moral implications of one's behavior on others (moral knowing and moral feeling). However, due to his lack of experience and minimal formal training as a coach, he may not feel competent to take moral action. Therefore, his ability to make decisions regarding ethical dilemmas may be limited.

Coach Lawson's Ethical Dilemma

After overhearing the conversation among the athletes about an upcoming activity involving the hazing of other athletes, Coach Lawson immediately experienced cognitive dissonance (conflicting or inconsistent thoughts) on how best to handle the situation. His cognitive dissonance was created by the conflict between moral and social character values. Coach Lawson knew that the hazing of another person demonstrates a lack of respect (moral character value) and he knew he had a responsibility (moral character value) to report what he had heard. However, Coach Lawson also felt a sense of loyalty (social character value) to uphold "the athlete code" he remembered well as an athlete and, thus, keep the information confidential. He may have also felt pressure to stay silent to protect the team's chances of winning (social character value) and avoid athletes missing games due to suspensions. Both values go against Coach Lawson's ability to take moral action and report the incident.

Ethical Decision-Making Questions

There are a variety of decision-making methods coaches can employ when making ethical decisions. However, generally they involve similar steps. Therefore, when faced with an ethical dilemma Coach Lawson can employ the following questions to help guide him in making a decision.

After recognizing the decision involves an ethical dilemma, ask these questions:

1. Who are the key stakeholders involved?
2. What are the moral character values involved?
3. What are the social character values involved?
4. What potential options do I have?
5. For each option, consider whether it aligns with the "good" (i.e., moral knowing). In other words, does it align with knowledge of

   - moral character values and their potential conflict with social character values?
   - my previous education and training?
   - perspective taking of stakeholders involved (implications of each action)?
   - my organization or coaching association's code of conduct?
   - current laws, policies, and/or regulations that may influence the dilemma?

6. For each option, consider whether it aligns with the "good" (i.e., moral) feeling. In other words, do I know what is "right" based on

   - my core values, personal mission, and coaching philosophy?
   - my past experiences?
   - what my ethical role models would do?

7. Choose an option and evaluate the decision. Does this option do "the good" (i.e., moral action)?

Improving Ethical Decision-Making Ability

The first step coaches take to improve their ability to make ethical decisions is to revisit what is important to them (i.e., personal values) and why they are coaching (see chapter 1). Second, coaches can clarify which of their values are social and moral character values to better identify when their values are in conflict and when they are faced with an ethical dilemma. Third, coaches can reflect on a recent scenario in which they were faced with an ethical dilemma. Using the questions above, coaches can evaluate how they made their decision and identify which factors (moral or social character values) may have played a role in their decision making. Lastly, using the same scenario, coaches can discuss with other coaches how they might have handled a similar situation. Through reflection, discussion, and a clearer understanding of how their values impact ethical decision making, coaches will improve their ability to make sound ethical decisions. To examine additional scenarios where coaches are challenged to make ethical decisions, review ethical scenarios 2 and 3. Then complete the questions provided. Consider how the ethical decision-making process is applied in each scenario.

ETHICAL SCENARIO 2: THE CLUB COACH AND PARENT PRESSURE

In mid-March, Sarah Bauer's U16 travel club softball team was one week into spring practice when all sports suddenly came to a halt due to a respiratory virus outbreak in the community. At first the parents were very concerned about the virus and advocated for the delayed start to the season. But after a few weeks of no practice, many of the parents were growing weary of the team possibly not being able to compete this coming summer. Some of their frustration stemmed from all the work the team had put in over the past year to be a contender for the U16 regional title. The U16 team operated independently of the other local clubs in the community and was 100 percent financially supported by the parents. Sarah received a small stipend for coaching each season.

As the first week of June approached, the parents grew restless. The virus outbreak seemed to be subsiding in the region. Anxious to get the team back together, one of the parents reached out to Sarah and stated, "It's time to start practice. The fields are open and we can implement physical distancing guidelines. Let's get everyone back together." Although Sarah was just as eager as the parents to get started again, she was unsure if it was the right time to bring the team back. She was still concerned about the spread of the virus and the challenge of running a practice while maintaining physical distancing and wearing masks. Nonetheless, parent pressure was mounting.

Questions to Consider:
1. What is driving the parents' decision to return to practice?
2. Why is Sarah conflicted about returning to practice?
3. What are the potential social and moral values in conflict in this scenario?
4. Should Sarah resume practices using appropriate protocols to provide a safe environment? Why or why not?

ETHICAL SCENARIO 3: THE PRIVATE SPORT COACH AND SPORTSMANSHIP

Brad Hampton is the owner/founder of the Elite Hoops Training Center, a private sport program that provides basketball skill and physical fitness for the top youth basketball players in his community. Brad is also the coach of the U18 Elite Hoops travel team and all the athletes on the team are members of the training center. For Brad, the Elite Hoops Training Center and coaching the club team is a full-time job. As a business owner he sells basketball and physical skill development. He also sells opportunity. Many of Brad's athletes have received college scholarships based on the exposure he provides through the travel team, as the Elite Hoops team attends all the top-level recruiting tournaments in the country. To train at the Elite Hoops Training Center and participate on the travel team is expensive, with parents spending thousands of dollars a year for their sons to train and play under Coach Hampton's guidance. Coach Hampton's coaching style is driven by his coaching philosophy, which is centered on challenging players to push themselves to go beyond what they believe they can accomplish. Therefore, Coach Hampton is tough-minded; he pushes the athletes on his team to be accountable to work hard in practice and when working out at the training center. This mind-set carries over on the court, as his team implements a full-court pressing defense to wear down the other team. Coach Hampton is often described as an intense coach. Even with his tough-minded approach, Coach Hampton respects the game of basketball and believes he has a duty to teach his athletes to honor the game and their opponent.

It was the third game of the day, late in the evening, and Elite Hoops was easily the dominant team as their opponent struggled to match their talent and intensity. Early in the second half with his team up by 30 points, Coach Hampton started looking to some of the younger players he had pulled up from the U16 team. But as he glanced down the bench he noticed both the head and assistant coach from State U walk into the gym. State U had been recruiting two of his starters over the last month. Although both players had played significant minutes in the first half, Coach Hampton knew the State U coaches were there to watch his two starters. He turned away from the bench and asked the official for a time-out.

Questions to Consider:

1. Should Coach Hampton substitute his two starters? Why or why not?
2. What obligation does Coach Hampton have to showcase his two starters for the State U coaches?
3. If Coach Hampton plays the two starters is he violating the concept of fair play?
4. Why do you think Coach Hampton might be conflicted about his decision in this scenario?

ETHICAL DECISION MAKING IN ACTION

There are a variety of decision-making methods coaches can employ when faced with ethical decisions. However, generally they involve similar steps. Therefore, when faced with an ethical dilemma, coaches can employ the ethical decision-making questions to help guide them in making a decision. Table 3.1 provides an example of how both Sarah and Brad can use the ethical decision-making questions to help them solve their ethical dilemma.

Table 3.1. Ethical Decision Making in Action

Decision-Making Questions	Sarah (softball coach)	Brad (basketball coach)
1. Who are the key stakeholders involved in this scenario?	Coaches, parents, and athletes	Coaches, parents, athletes, and collegiate recruiters
2. What are the moral character values involved in this scenario?	Respect, responsibility, and beneficence	Respect, responsibility, and fair play
3. What are the social character values involved in this scenario?	Winning and commitment	Success
4. What potential options do I have?	a) Resume team practices and align with the parent's wishes. b) Continue to suspend current team practices, knowing that the parents may remove her as a team coach. c) Begin a modified team practice schedule.	a) Play the two starters and run up the score. b) Sit the two starters to demonstrate respect to the other team. c) Play the two starters, but not at the same time.

(continued)

Table 3.1. *Continued*

Decision-Making Questions	Sarah (softball coach)	Brad (basketball coach)
5. For each option consider whether it aligns with the "good" (i.e., moral knowing)?	a) The athletes will get back on the field and get to play with their teammates. Bringing the athletes back early could be risking the health and safety of the athletes, creating potential harm. b) By waiting, Sarah gives herself more time to determine how to best proceed safely. Both the parents and the athletes may continue to put pressure on her to start practice and she might be replaced by another coach that agrees with the parents. c) By taking the middle ground Sarah keeps her position as coach and the athletes return to play, but is Sarah fulfilling her responsibility to provide a safe environment.	a) The team will win the game and assert their dominance, but this action demonstrates a lack of respect for the norms of the game and the concept of fair play. b) While this approach demonstrates respect and fair play toward the opponent, is Brad fulfilling his promise (i.e., responsibility) to his athletes to help them acquire athletic scholarships. c) This approach demonstrates respect for the game and allows Brad to meet his responsibility to help his athletes acquire a collegiate scholarship at the same time, but does it still disrespect the game?
6. For each option consider whether it aligns with the "good" (i.e., moral feeling)?	Both Sarah and Brad reflect on their personal core values, personal mission statement, and coaching philosophy relative to each of the options.	
7. Choose an option. Does this option do "the good" (i.e., moral action)?	Both Sarah and Brad select an option and then reflect one more time to ensure the option is the decision they want to make and the best course of moral action.	

IN ACTION

CHARACTER EDUCATION FOR COACHES

In our athletic program we are thoughtful and purposeful in how we hire coaches. We implement a focused evaluation system where we strive to ensure that our entire coaching staff will role model ethical behavior. Part of being a coach at Tumwater involves taking part in a character-based leadership program that outlines our expectations and gives us an opportunity to observe leadership behaviors in action. For example, I can observe our coaches teaching, modeling, and demonstrating the character expectations we have established for our athletic programs, which include trust, servant leadership, respect, commitment, kindness, and grit. We reinforce these character traits using NGUNNGU (Never-Give-Up-Never-Never-Give-Up attitude). Each of these traits has authentic scenarios that place both the athlete and the coach into situations where they need to make ethical decisions and at the same time allows us an opportunity to reflect and refine those decisions. Many of the scenarios involve coaches working with the athlete, while others are related to the administrative evaluation processes. As an athletic administrator, I make sure to observe individual programs in meetings, practices, and games to gain a sense of appropriate decision making in action that aligns with our character expectations. Also, I have found that by observing coaches and athletes, they welcome this interaction and it helps to build a trusting and inviting relationship between our athletic administration and our coaching staff. In the end, we want coaches at Tumwater High School to serve as role models, be student centered, stay focused on teaching life-related lessons, and provide a positive experience.

—Tim Graham, athletic director, Tumwater High School (WA)

TEACHING AND REINFORCING ETHICAL BEHAVIOR AMONG ATHLETES

As noted in the previous scenarios, coaches serve as key role models to help athletes recognize how to act in ethical ways and how to make ethical decisions. However, coaches can engage in additional actions to aid athletes in developing their own ethical mind-set. Researchers have noted that discussing ethical dilemmas[11] and reinforcing ethical behavior[12] can influence moral reasoning, intentions, and behaviors among athletes.

Discussing Ethical Dilemmas

Discussing ethical dilemmas in the youth sport setting involves recognizing or creating teachable moments and discussing them with athletes. Coaches can be on the lookout for sport situations where coaches and/or athletes did or did not engage in fair play, respectful behavior, or integrity. When identified, coaches bring these situations to the attention of their athletes and discuss why it is a good or bad behavior. If poor behavior is identified, then the coach could discuss how it could be handled differently in the future. The following three examples highlight how a tennis coach might use this method with their athletes.

In the first example, the coach could find a teachable moment specific to tennis. In 2018, Swiss tennis player, Roger Federer, made a call for all professional tennis players to be respectful toward the ball boys and ball girls during tournaments.[13] A former ball boy himself, he noted that they represent the future of tennis and are due respect. A tennis coach, Coach Fry, could describe the scenario to the team and ask why it is an example of good sport conduct. For example, Coach Fry could ask why it is important to be respectful and how they, as tennis players, can show respect during their matches. With encouragement, hopefully, the athletes will note ways to be respectful toward the opponent, the officials, and the people that maintain and run the tennis facilities.

A tennis coach could also look for teachable moments during competitions. During a recent tennis tournament, a top player, Mahala, was competing against a strong opponent, Maggie. She had lost to Maggie on multiple occasions during the past year. However, Mahala had been improving her tennis game and working on her upper body and core strength. She felt ready to compete against Maggie in the tournament. During the finals, they were both performing well, but Mahala was maintaining a small lead. It was a match point for Mahala and she hit an ace to the deep left corner of the court pulling out a great upset to defeat Maggie. As soon as the point occurred Maggie looked shocked. Then an angry look came across her face as she threw her tennis racquet into the fence and walked away without congratulating Mahala. Everyone was shocked. The tennis coach, Coach Newton, brings the team together and begins by congratulating Mahala and pointing out how her effort, focus, power shots, and use of strategy during the match were noticeable and played a key role in helping her achieve the victory today. Also, using Maggie's response as an example, Coach Newton points to her poor behavior. Coach Newton notes how it is difficult to lose and athletes can often become emotional and make the mistake that Maggie did. But, she also points out that part of being a good sport is learning to control one's emotions and losing with grace. Coach Newton continues and asks her athletes about the different ways they can control their emotions. Additionally, Coach Newton asks why it is important to be respectful to the opponent and ways to do so when they lose. Lastly, she reminds the athletes that having a challenging competitor makes you a better player, highlighting how Mahala was challenged by Maggie over the years to become a better player, which she clearly had demonstrated during the tournament. Coach Newton concludes with a statement about why it was such a great match, as both players were playing good tennis and she hopes Maggie will realize that she is still a good tennis player.

Coaches can also create teachable moments in practice. Coach Olivia Sidoti has noticed that her tennis players (ages 9–12) are focusing more on winning than on improving their tennis game by calling balls out, even though they were on the line. She decides to create a series of quick games meant for six players. Players earn points the traditional way but also by accurately calling a ball out or executing correct form during a tennis stroke. Two players play against one another, two players serve as line judges to verify points are called fairly, and two players watch strokes. The point system is as follows:

- one point is awarded when a ball is accurately called out and verified by the line judges,
- one point is awarded when a player demonstrates good form for their stroke observed by the two players watching strokes using the assessment system created by Coach Sidoti, and
- one point is awarded for scoring a tennis point as scored in competition.

After each eight-point game, players rotate positions in a round-robin format until a winner is declared. Following the game, Coach Sidoti brings the players together to discuss what they learned during the game and why there was a focus on form and making calls. Hopefully, the players will recognize that what makes for successful play is good form and fair play.

Reinforcing Ethical Behavior

Another action coaches can take to encourage fair play, respect, and integrity is to reinforce this behavior when they see their athletes exhibit it. The best way coaches can do this is by providing feedback. When coaches see an athlete extend a hand to a fallen player during a soccer game, they can provide positive feedback. For example, the coach could say, "Mikala, thanks for taking the time to help a player up after the fall. That is really what it means to be a good teammate." Or if a youth volleyball coach notices players leaving the gym without putting away volleyballs, cones, paper wrappers from snacks, or leaving empty water bottles, the coach can provide a reminder about respecting the facility where they play by leaving it the way it was before they came. Coaches can also encourage athletes to provide each other feedback. For example, at the end of practice a field hockey coach might ask players to highlight players who demonstrated respect and fair play during the small-sided games and scrimmages that day. By discussing ethical dilemmas associated with good or poor sport conduct, reinforcing good ethical behavior, and pointing out why poor behavior is unacceptable, coaches set the stage for their athletes to continue to develop their own ethical mind-set.

IN ACTION

DEVELOPING POSITIVE PERSONAL CHARACTER TRAITS

As a coach, I first try to get to know each one of my student-athletes and build a positive relationship with them. I demonstrate that I care just as much about my slowest runner as I care about my fastest runner, by taking an interest in their lives, hobbies, and interests. I believe this builds trust and lets them know that I truly care about them and not just about what they can contribute athletically. This also creates an all-around better environment because our team becomes like a family. After relationships are built, it becomes easier to teach life lessons and build character. I can teach specific examples of how the character traits apply to their life. In cross country, we stress important character traits, such as work ethic, determination, and accountability. All of which apply directly to being successful in many other aspects of life. As a role model, I also try to lead by example. I expect our kids to represent our team and school in a very positive manner, and that starts with me. I would never ask a student-athlete to do anything I would not be willing to do myself.

—Brett Rinehart, head cross country
coach, Chanute High School (KS)

CONCLUSION

Athletes are influenced by the actions and the words of their coaches. If coaches model positive and ethical behavior, then the youth under their guidance will have the potential to learn about ethical practice and good sport conduct through sport participation. Thus, serving in the position of coach carries with it the responsibility to act in an ethical manner. In addition, the culture of youth sport creates a variety of ethical scenarios, as noted in this chapter, that challenge coaches' ability to make ethical decisions. Developing an ethical mind-set and decision-making framework and teaching and reinforcing athletes' ethical behavior help coaches handle these challenges and learning opportunities.

COACH TIPS!

- Reflect on a decision made in the past and consider how moral knowledge, moral feeling, and moral action may have played a role in the final decision. Consider how this decision may be different now given experiences since the past decision.

- Revisit the list of personal values often and learn to recognize an ethical dilemma based on a conflict of values.
- Utilize the ethical decision-making checklist when faced with a current ethical dilemma.
- Look for teachable moments in practice sessions and in competition to reinforce positive behavior or redirect negative behavior.

COACH DEVELOPER TIPS!

- Create a coach development plan for the coaches that encourages reflection on their ethical mind-set and assists coaches in recognizing teachable moments during practice and in competitive settings.
- Provide feedback and support to coaches using the ethical decision-making checklist after they have faced an ethical dilemma.
- Share and/or discuss recent ethical dilemmas with the coaching staff to discuss how best to handle them within the sport organization.

4

To Coach Is to
Build Relationships

Consider the typical day for sport coaches. They usually check in with administrators about the facility and equipment updates. They greet their athletes, share with them the practice plan, and provide instruction and feedback throughout the practice. They interact with parents dropping off or picking up their kids from practice. They communicate with officials, assistant coaches, sports medicine professionals, and other staff members in preparing for practices and competitions. A day in the life of a coach is filled with opportunities to connect with others and foster positive relationships.

CONNECT WITH OTHERS

When you ask coaches, what is the most rewarding part of coaching, many coaches will talk about the relationships that they developed with their athletes. Coach Dean Smith, former University of North Carolina basketball coach and winner of three NCAA Division I men's basketball national championships, put it this way:

> The most important thing in good leadership is truly caring. The best leaders in any profession care about the people they lead, and the people who are being led know when the caring is genuine and when it's faked or not there at all. I was a demanding coach, but my players knew that I cared for them and that my caring didn't stop when they graduated and went off to their careers.[1] . . . If you develop a close relationship with a player, as we did, you don't drop it just

because the player's eligibility is up. You don't forget them. I wanted to stay in touch, and I'm always pleased, thrilled, and interested when our former players let me know what's going on in their lives.[2]

For Coach Smith, developing a positive relationship meant caring for the whole person, not just their athletic capabilities, over time. Coach-athlete relationships—really, all relationships—are defined by the sharing and shaping of each other's thoughts, behaviors, and emotions.[3] There are many ways that coaches create positive relationships with their athletes. Sophia Jowett and Vaithehy Shanmugam,[4] in reviewing research on the coach-athlete relationship, found that when athletes indicate having a good relationship with their coach, they also report feeling more motivated, passionate, and connected to teammates. In reviewing work on the caring climate, Mary Fry and E. Whitney Moore[5] observed that when athletes perceive the climate to be caring, they report greater enjoyment, commitment to their sport, willingness to help and care for others, and liking of teammates and coaches. For Coach Smith, it is clear that just being in the relationship and hearing from his athletes was rewarding—a sentiment that is supported by coaches in all sport settings, including youth sport.

TIPS FOR CONNECTING WITH OTHERS

So how do coaches create positive relationships? Researchers and practitioners have provided insight. Jowett and Shanmugam[6] suggest that coaches can engage in relational coaching. Relational coaching involves coaches developing close, trusting, respectful, and collaborative long-term relationships with their athletes. Thus, coaches get to know their athletes, seek to be responsive to their needs, and work with them to develop both in sport and as people. Daniel Rhind and Jowett[7] report that coaches maintain positive relationships when they manage conflict well, get to know their athletes beyond just the sport, seek to motivate athletes, and support their development in a positive way. In addition, Fry and colleagues[8] recommend that coaches foster a caring climate by creating a welcoming, safe, and respectful environment where athletes are heard and supported by the coach and teammates. They encourage coaches to model respectful, kind, supportive, and welcoming behaviors, thus, creating a community of caring where athletes, family members, and staff get to know one another and recognize the value of each member of the team, while also recognizing their role in supporting one another. Based on this work, several

Table 4.1.   Ways to Connect with Others

a) Commit: Commit to creating positive relationships with all athletes.
b) Engage: Engage in appropriate interactions (friendly, honest, and respectful but understand role as leader/adult).
c) Welcome: Present a welcoming atmosphere for all people on the team.
d) Familiarize: Get to know all athletes and help them to get to know each other.
e) Be present: Be there for each athlete by being responsive and listening.
f) Empathize: Take an empathic approach and seek to understand before taking action.
g) Recognize potential: Help athletes meet their role on the team by helping them improve individually, believing in them and their potential, and using their strengths to assist the team.
h) Support: Support athletes' holistic development (physical, technical, psychological, social).
i) Appreciate: Show appreciation toward all athletes and their role on the team (value each person).
j) Collaborate: Cooperate with all team members by seeking feedback about how the team can get better. Involve athletes in the decision-making process and encourage their participation.
k) Encourage: Help athletes to be supportive of one another.
l) Resolution: Manage conflict effectively.

strategies are highlighted in how coaches can integrate connecting with others into coaching practice (see table 4.1). In addition, an example of how one coach, Coach Martin, works to connect with others is highlighted below with key concepts from table 4.1 placed in parentheses and bolded text.

COACH MARTIN'S STORY

That morning, Coach Martin, the high school volleyball coach, sends a "good morning" text to her assistant coach and reminds her to show up 10 minutes before practice to set up the courts. She also texts Kathy Gibson and John Kim to thank them for signing up to run concessions at the game tomorrow night and reminding them what time to be there (**appreciate**). She then sends her *happy day* quote to her players through the team app. She includes a reminder about 3:30 p.m. practice that day (**commit, engage**).

Coach Martin arrives at the school at 2:30 p.m. to check in with the athletic director, Anna Marset, about tomorrow's home match. She sees the athletic director and asks, "Anna, how are you doing?" (**engage**).

Anna responds and then engages in a short conversation with Coach Martin about the recent field hockey game. "It is great to hear that the field hockey team is really developing this year," states Coach Martin. "I just wanted to let you know that the Gibsons and Kims are going to help at the concession stand for tomorrow's match. I also touched base with the visiting team coach and they plan to arrive around 4:15 p.m. How are things on your end?" (**be present**, *PITCH it*, *listen*, *observe*).

"Going great," states Anna. "I am really looking forward to your match tomorrow."

"Thanks for getting things organized," says Coach Martin. "Will you be able to join us? (**appreciate, engage**).

"Yes," says Anna, "I will be there" (*listen*).

"Fantastic, we appreciate your support," exclaims Coach Martin, "Let me know if I can help with any other preparations" (**appreciate**).

On her way to the gym, Coach Martin checks in with a teacher about one of her players, Mona, who is having some academic struggles in class (**support**).

At the gym, she sees Coach Cook setting up for practice, including posting the practice plan in several key spots in the gym. Together, they review the practice plan and Coach Martin encourages Coach Cook to use her expertise to lead the section of practice on serving (**collaborate, encourage**).

As they are talking, two seniors walk in with their music selection for practice. Coach Martin thanks them for bringing the tunes to get everyone revved up for tomorrow's match and starts the music as team members stream in from the locker room. Both Coach Cook and Coach Martin greet players as they begin the senior-led warm-up, checking in with players to see how things are going (**appreciate, engage, welcome**).

Coach Cook says, "Frances, tell us how the cello concert went." After her explanation, Coach Martin chimes in with, "Well done, Frances. You will have to bring in a sample of your music to share during practice" (**engage, familiarize, support**).

Coach Martin also seeks out Mona to say she has chatted with her teacher and she has a plan she wants to share after practice (**engage**).

After warm-up, Coach Martin pulls the team together. "Great to see everyone today!" she states. "Thank you Casey and Tina for leading warm-up (**appreciate**). As I mentioned yesterday, we are going to work on our plan for tomorrow's match. Remember, the key for today is focus. Focus during serving, digging, and passing (*PITCH it*). Okay, we will start with serves and then on to turn and dig. Everyone in on three. Go team! Focus!" (**support**).

As practice progresses, Coach Cook and Coach Martin remind them of the purpose for each drill and game. They both circulate around the court and among the players to provide necessary feedback (**engage, recognize potential**).

"Sam, I love how you are placing the ball for your serve," says Coach Martin. "However, I think you can get more power by swinging that arm a bit more. Let me show you." [She shows the athelete the incorrect form and then follows up with correct form.] "Okay, you give it a try," states Coach Martin. Then she follows up a successful attempt by Sam with a high five (**appreciate, engage, recognize potential**).

Next, Coach Martin catches Nadia exhibiting good focus and maintaining high energy during practice. "Nadia, nice placement for that pass, way to focus on play and getting it over the net," exclaims Coach Martin. "You are making such good progress. I like the hustle as you follow the ball over the net. That is going to pay off big tomorrow" (**appreciate, engage, recognize potential**).

Practice concludes and Coach Martin pulls the team together. Coach Martin comments on their energy and focus and then turns to Jen. "Jen, you nailed the turn and dig drill today. Nice focus," says Coach Martin. "Tabitha, your ability to accurately pass to your mates was on; I look forward to seeing what will happen tomorrow. And Deja, great setting and communication during the scrimmage. I love the support." Coach Martin continues, "There is just not enough time to name everyone, but take a moment and turn to someone near you and highlight what you saw today in practice" (**appreciate, engage, recognize potential, support**).

After giving them a chance to communicate with each other, Coach Marten exclaims, "Wonderful! This is the support, energy, and focus we need for tomorrow's match. Remember, be here tomorrow at 4:30 p.m. I will send you the "to-do" list and "must-bring" list via our team app. Okay, juniors take us out on your cheer" (listen, check for understanding, **support**).

Following practice, Coach Martin touches base with Mona. "Mona, thank you for staying after practice to talk with me for a few minutes. I saw your math grade and your teacher reached out to me regarding your performance. It seems like you are really struggling" (**be present, engage, support**).

Mona acknowledges her struggles and is embarrassed about her performance. She tells Coach Martin that she has never been good at math and the new material is just confusing (**be present**, listen).

"Mona, I know this must be frustrating for you and that you are trying to do your best. You know we all have those things we struggle with," says Coach Martin (**engage, support, empathize**). "For me, it was English literature. I had a difficult time grasping concepts and writing essays. However, what helped me was getting a tutor and practicing it more often. I am wondering if that might help you? (*PITCH it, observe, use EI*).

Mona acknowledges she could use more help but cannot afford a tutor, and she has to go to work after practices (*listen, observe*). "I thought that might be the case," says Coach Martin (**engage, support**). "Therefore, Ms. Thornton and I looked at other times during the day. Turns out that she has some time during your study period. She can give you some guided practice assignments that you can work on during your study period and she will come in and walk through them with you. Not every study period, but twice a week to start. How does that sound?" (*PITCH it*).

After meeting with Mona, Coach Martin and Coach Cook have their 15-minute, end-of-practice reflection. Coach Martin thanks Coach Cook for taking the lead on the serving drills and her help with providing timely feedback to the athletes (**appreciate**). Coach Cook remarks that they really got the message related to focus today. Together, they refine the plan for the next day's match (**collaborate, recognize potential**).

Coach Martin: Connecting with Others

Coach Martin's story demonstrates the many ways that coaches are intentional about connecting with others using a variety of the strategies (see table 4.1). Coach Martin is intentional about developing relationships with multiple stakeholders. Most critically, she is trying to make connections with all athletes rather than those that may be outgoing, more talented, love the sport, or share a similar personality. By planning ahead, Coach Martin has time to greet her athletes as they enter the court and during the warm-ups. Both Coach Cook and Coach Martin demonstrate their support for athlete development by providing constructive feedback, supporting them during practice and encouraging them to support one another. Also, they recognize and support athletes' strengths (e.g., playing cello) and weaknesses (e.g., math) outside of sport. Coach Martin demonstrates appreciation for her athletes and staff throughout the day. She clearly values their contributions (e.g., effort and focus in practice, team support) and finds ways for everyone to take part (e.g., seniors leading warm-ups, juniors leading cheer). Coach Martin also acts with empathy as she helps Mona deal with her academic struggles and she further listens to Mona and recognizes her potential to be better.

REFLECTING ON CONNECTING WITH OTHERS

While Coach Martin's story represents one version of an exemplary coach in action, there are multiple ways and styles for coaches to connect with others. Coaches can use the following questions to consider how they can better connect with others.

1. Do I seek to connect with all athletes on the team? If not, why are there differences and how could I connect better with all athletes, even if the connection is deeper with some athletes?
2. What times during and outside of practice can I use for connecting with others?
3. What strategies noted do I want to work on? What are some concrete ways that I can implement them in my practice? For example, I want to be more welcoming by starting every practice with a consistent greeting, like "Great to see everyone today."
4. Are there obstacles that get in the way of my ability to connect with others, such as lack of time, athlete personality, my own personality, or lack of skills? Are there ways that I could overcome these obstacles to help me develop better relationships?

IN ACTION

CONNECTING WITH ATHLETES

I make a concerted effort to show all the players in my program that I care for them. Being a head basketball coach in high school, I don't get to work as much with the freshman and junior varsity team as I would like. Therefore, to connect with those athletes, I will reach out to multiple athletes throughout the week during their practice time. I want them to feel like they are a part of our program. During my conversation with them, I try to get them to crack a smile and thank them for being at practice. When it comes

(continued)

to my varsity team, I am able to talk with them daily and build relationships a lot quicker. One approach I use to build relationships with my players is to have "check-in" time with them. I ask them what they think is going well for them on the court, what they need help on, and what is a goal they have for themselves. This typically leads into great conversation where I can show tremendous support for that player, push them to become better, and hold them accountable to their goals. By building great relationships with my athletes, they want to come to open gyms, attend training sessions in the weight room, and become a part of our team.

—Manny Melo, head boys' basketball coach,
Battleground High School (WA)

IN ACTION

MAKING CONNECTIONS IS A COMMITMENT

Coaches must love the kids they coach; you cannot fake this. Kids can tell about 1,000 miles off if you truly care for them or not. Without this commitment all athletic-related goals pale in comparison. I have challenged our coaches to be the type of coach that gets invited to weddings. That is a life on life commitment that goes from the tips of their toes to the tops of their heads. It is not enough to model love, the coach must tell them fairly often, too. If we are only about technique and tactics we will never achieve the depth of relationship and connection that is needed to assist our athletes in being their best on and off the field of play. Relationships are the literal glue that assist coaches in connecting deeply with our athletes and bring them to a place where they are willing to push past failure, challenges at home, and obstacles in peer relationship to excel.

—Kevin M. Bryant, interscholastic athletic administrator,
Thrive Athletic Consulting (OR)

DEVELOP INTERPERSONAL SKILLS

Another aspect of building strong relationships is the ability to use good skill-ful interactions with others.[9] The use of interpersonal skills has been shown to have positive outcomes for motivation, commitment, teamwork, and per-formance.[10] While there are many skills needed for interacting with others in the sport context, such as self-confidence, assertiveness, and problem solving, this section will focus on communication skills and emotional intelligence. More specifically, sending clear and concise messages, engaging in active lis-tening, using good observational skills, and developing emotional intelligence are reviewed (see table 4.2). In addition, the previous story with Coach Martin highlights how key interpersonal skills provided in table 4.2 are applied in practice. These key concepts are in parentheses and italicized.

Table 4.2. Ways to Develop Interpersonal Skills

1. PITCH it	Use this approach to send clear and concise messages that are • productive • informative • timed well • consistent • honest
2. Check for understanding	Check in to see if a message was received and confirm • was the message accurately received? • was its intent interpreted correctly? • did the receiver execute the message the way you intended?
3. Listen	Engage in active listening skills to • be present • seek to learn • check for understanding • be responsive
4. Observe	Use good observational skills
5. Use emotional intelligence (EI)	Demonstrate the skills of emotional intelligence, such as • be aware of own emotions, their triggers, and impact on others • engage in good emotional control • consider the thoughts and feelings of others (be empathetic) • use good social skills

SENDING CLEAR AND CONCISE MESSAGES

A skill that everyone could work on is developing their ability to create and send clear and concise messages. Robin Vealey[11] provides a "PITCH it" acro-nym for creating messages that are productive, informative, timed well, consis-tent, and honest. *Productive* messages are positive, align verbal and nonverbal communication, have the right emotional tone, and consider the audience and context so as to be received by the intended audience. *Informative* messages are concise and contain specific content that is helpful to the receiver. *Timed well* messages are those that are given at the right time and place so that they are received properly by the athlete. *Consistent* messages are those that reinforce core values of the team and are contingent on performance. *Honest* messages are authentic to the person and do not represent hidden agendas or mixed messages. When sending PITCH it messages it is also important to check in to see if the message was accurately received and executed as intended.

Coach Martin: Sending Clear and Concise Messages

Coach Martin's story provides insight into how these skills can be effectively applied in practice. Coach Martin creates and sends effective messages using multiple modes of communication. She follows Vealey's[12] "PITCH it" acronym by creating team speeches that are productive, informative, timed well, consistent, and honest. Additionally, her feedback statements are PITCHed well and she times her messages with Mona so as not to put her on the spot regarding her academic struggle. She also makes sure her messages are accurately received and executed. For example, she texted the assistant coach and parents, checked in with the athletic director, and asked players to provide positive feedback to their teammates on where they saw focus and support during practice. The variety of means she uses to check in with her athletes suggest that there are multiple modes of communication to PITCH a message.

ENGAGING ACTIVE LISTENING

People often assume that listening is the easy part of the communication process. However, listening is not easy work. Listening requires coaches to direct their undivided attention toward the other, process verbal and nonverbal communication, check in with the person to make sure they have understood the message, and then craft a response or enact a behavior based on what they have heard. Critical to listening is learning from the person sharing the message—learning what message they are trying to communicate, learning what they need, and learning what knowledge they have to offer. Therefore, active listening requires coaches to be present by attending to the other, seek to learn what the other has to say, check their understanding of what was said, and be responsive in thought, feeling, and/or action.

Coach Martin: Engaging in Active Listening

Coach Martin uses her active listening skills with the athletic director, teacher, assistant coach, and athletes to help her understand their perspective and respond in ways to support them and/or learn from them. However, the best example is when Coach Martin is talking with Mona. She attends to her concerns about her struggles with math. She lets Mona know that she has heard her frustration and her concerns by noting those to Mona. She also is responsive in feeling and thought. Additionally, because she has done some initial planning for this conversation, she is ready to take action to help Mona.

USING GOOD OBSERVATIONAL SKILLS

Another key component of good communication is combining active listening with good observational skills. By observing body language, team interactions, athlete outcomes, or athlete performance, coaches can learn a lot about what might be going on with their athletes. However, it is important to follow up observations with questions and active listening to avoid assumptions or misrepresentations. See how Coach Wagner puts this into practice.

Coach Wagner's Observational Skills

The basketball bounced toward the baseline. Allie, a 13-year-old eighth grader at East Lookout Middle School, chased the ball. Her pace is slower than normal. Allie's effort caught the attention of her coach, Emily Wagner. Coach Wagner was accustomed to Allie's competitiveness and speed during practice sessions. Allie could move from one position on the court to another position faster than any other girl on the team. An explosive trait and an important one in the sport of basketball. But in this moment, Allie lacked any type of explosive action. The ball reached the sideline ahead of her, the last bounce splitting the sideline, half in and half out. Allie's shoulders slumped as her stride slowed. She turned back toward the court, her face reflecting frustration. Coach Wagner recognizes something was off with Allie. She turns the practice over to her assistant coach and pulls Allie over to the side of the court. Coach Wagner says, "Allie, I have noticed that your speed is a little off today. Is everything alright?" Allie responds that she has been feeling really tired the last couple of days and she does not seem to have the energy on the court. Coach Wagner follows up with a few more questions regarding Allie's physical state and her other extracurricular activities and they conclude that she is in need of some rest to let her body recuperate.

Coach Wagner: Using Observational Skills and Active Listening

Coach Wagner notices Allie's change in demeanor and actions and uses them as an opportunity for connection and communication. By starting with what she has noticed and asking if Allie is alright, Coach Wagner is seeking to understand rather than blaming the athlete. For example, Coach Wagner did not jump to the conclusion that Allie was slacking and blame her for not giving her best effort. By seeking to understand, Coach Wagner learned the underlying cause of her actions and together they developed a plan for her to recover. This also reinforced Coach Wagner's commitment to help Allie. This example highlights how Coach Wagner was in control of her emotions and sought to empathize with her player, demonstrating key components of emotional intelligence.

DEVELOPING EMOTIONAL INTELLIGENCE

Daniel Goleman[13] noted that an important skill for leaders to develop is their emotional intelligence. Emotional intelligence is the ability for an individual to be aware of and manage their own emotions, understand the emotions of others, and use this awareness and understanding to guide behavior and thinking. Goleman asserts that emotionally intelligent leaders engage in four main tasks: (1) develop awareness of their emotions, what triggers certain emotions, and how one's emotions influence others, (2) regulate their own emotions, (3) become more empathetic so as to understand and feel the emotions of others, and (4) use social skills. In the following example, learn how developing emotional intelligence might help Coach Beeler.

Coach Beeler and Emotional Intelligence

Sarah Beeler, a U14 club volleyball coach, could feel the set slipping away. It was the seventh match of the weekend and the last day of the tournament. Her team had competed hard the entire tournament, a trait that matched Coach Beeler's leadership style. This match was no different. In this particular set, the team raced to an 11–1 lead, but the opponent started to rally, scoring 13 consecutive points. With each point, the players could sense Coach Beeler's frustration level rise. Beeler was an enthusiastic, passionate, and competitive coach, earning her athlete's respect with her knowledge of the game and willingness to help them improve their volleyball skills. But on occasion, her competitiveness went a little too far and she could erupt at the team, individual athletes, and the officials. As the opponent continued to increase their lead, the athletes started glancing over at Coach Beeler to see how she would react. Just at that point, Coach Beeler lost it and began yelling at the players on the court for their performance.

Coach Beeler: A Need to Develop Emotional Intelligence

First, it is not clear that Coach Beeler recognized her emotional response or the negative impact that her frustration was having on her players. It could very well be that her inability to recognize this could have led the players to be more apprehensive as they waited for her to erupt in anger. Second, it is clear that Coach Beeler did not control her emotions or use appropriate social skills as she "*lost it*" and chose to yell at her players leading to disruptive and harmful behavior for her players, parents, and fans. Third, she did not consider her players' feelings about their current situation and what they needed from her to be successful in a close set (i.e., 11–14). Coach Beeler and her team would both benefit if she worked on developing her emotional intelligence.

REFLECTING ON DEVELOPING INTERPERSONAL SKILLS

In sum, developing interpersonal skills will improve coaches' relationships with athletes, parents, administrators, and the community in which they work. In this section, several ways that coaches can improve their communication skills and emotional intelligence were highlighted. Coaches may want to consider the following questions in developing their own interpersonal skills.

1. What interpersonal skills do I need to work on most to help me build more positive relationships? Examples of interpersonal skills include communication, conflict resolution, negotiation, emotional intelligence, problem solving, self-confidence, cultural competence, and cooperation.
2. Videotape a practice and consider the following:

    a. Was communication clear and concise?

    b. Did my messages get interpreted correctly?

    c. Did I use my observational skills to pick up on how the athletes were performing and interacting with one another?

    d. Did I listen to my athletes?

3. What is my emotional intelligence? Am I aware of my emotions and how they affect others? Do I know what triggers my anger, anxiety, excitement,

and happiness? Can I control my emotions when needed? Do I seek to understand others' feelings and perspectives?

CONCLUSION

Building relationships in sport is an important endeavor. Within this chapter, connecting with others and developing interpersonal skills are highlighted as strategies for developing stronger relationships. By reviewing this content and considering the reflective questions and tips, coaches can continue to work on this valuable skill.

COACH TIPS!

- Seek opportunities to reach out and connect with athletes. Take advantage of the time before practice, after practice, waiting for a bus, or waiting for parent pick-up.
- Discover why athletes are playing. Understanding their why can help create better connections.
- Communicate in short, clear, and concise messages when providing instruction and/or feedback.
- Learn to ask great questions to generate dialogue and pause to listen to improve communication with others.
- Develop scenarios within practice sessions that provide opportunities to implement communication strategies and better connect with others.

COACH DEVELOPER TIPS!

- Observe coaches interacting with athletes and consider providing support for video technology to give them the ability to see themselves in action.
- Provide resources for coaches on active listening, observational skills, emotional intelligence, and interpersonal skills while also challenging them to seek more information on their own.
- Assist the coach in learning self-reflection techniques, including emotional intelligence.
- Implement PITCH it or similar type strategies into coach orientation sessions and training programs.
- Evaluate the coach's progress in building relationships by asking indirect questions of the athletes under their guidance.

5

To Coach Is to
Set the Climate

Jim White, a successful high school cross country coach in Central California for 22 years (1980 to 2002), led McFarland High School to 9 state championships, 15 sectional titles, and 22 league championships.[1] McFarland is a predominantly Hispanic/Latinx community where a large majority of the population is employed in agriculture (working in the fields). Coach White, who is white and is affectionately called *Blanco* by his athletes, established a culture within his cross country program that encouraged participation and challenged each athlete to get better while supporting each other. As the story is told, Coach White purposefully found ways to connect with his athletes, using sport to expose them to a world outside of McFarland. For example, he took them to see the ocean, camping in Yosemite, and competitions in New York, Germany, and China.[2] The environment that Coach White created was driven by his approach to coaching (coaching philosophy) and coaching style (see chapter 1). In short, Coach White cared about his athletes and he role modeled this approach in his daily actions and conversations with his team. Using this approach, he created an environment within his program where athletes wanted to be a part of the team.

In sport, the actions of the coach create a setting that either nurtures, hinders, or fails to help athletes and/or the team develop and reach their full potential. In examining the story about Coach White, it seems clear that he was successful in establishing a team climate to match the expectations of working as a high school coach in the sport of cross country. By connecting with each athlete, Coach White established a welcoming environment for each member of the cross country team, while at the same time challenging them to reach their potential. By being clear in his purpose as a coach and demonstrating this through his actions, his athletes became more comfortable with him. In turn, being a member of the cross country team became a safe space for athletes to be challenged, to test themselves, and learn from mistakes. In essence, he used a variety of coaching practices to develop a positive and inclusive sport environment. The following three coaching scenarios provide insight into how coaches can implement positive and inclusive coaching practices in their own teams.

SCENARIO 1: PATRICK THE COMMUNITY VOLUNTEER PARENT COACH

Patrick tapped his fingers on the steering column, impatiently, as his car inched forward in procession toward his son Sam's elementary school pick-up location. He heard a bell ring and kids began spilling out of the building. Sam, a fifth grader, was well versed in the routine on where to meet his father for a ride after school. Sam bounded into the backseat and began speaking to his father at a feverish pace. He shared a couple items about his day and then blurted out, "Dad, did you hear anything about when flag football starts?"

"Not yet," stated Patrick. "I am sure the parks and recreation office will be in touch with us soon."

Sam responded, "Are you going to coach my team this year?"

"Probably not," said Patrick. "They likely already have the coaches lined up."

That same evening, Patrick's phone started buzzing. He did not recognize the number but noticed it was local and took the call.

"Good evening sir, this is Kylie from Parks and Rec," stated the caller. "I am calling about our flag football program. Your son, Sam has been placed on the Lions team."

"Great," said Patrick. "He is really excited about the season starting."

Kylie continued, "Sir, would you like to serve as the team coach? We do not currently have a coach for his team."

Patrick did not respond right away, as he was a bit surprised by the request. He had volunteered once to coach Sam's T-ball team, but he had never played organized football, and, beyond the occasional social outing to a local collegiate football game, he rarely watched the sport.

Kylie, sensing his hesitancy went into her sales pitch, "Sir, if we are unable to find a coach we may not be able to field his team in the league and I have already asked a number of parents. We have a two-hour coaches meeting next week with more information and we have a lot of returning coaches that can help you get started."

Although still hesitant, but sold by the sales pitch or threat of no opportunity for his son, Patrick responded, "Okay, I will do it."

"Great," exclaimed Kylie. "The coaches meeting is next Monday and practices begin on Thursday."

Patrick hung up the phone and thought, what did I just agree to? Patrick remembered from coaching T-ball how difficult it could be to get the kids organized and stay focused while trying to teach the game. With T-ball, he had experience playing baseball and knew what skills to teach, but football involves more strategy. He knew Sam would be excited about him coaching the team. However, Patrick felt unprepared and now a bit anxious. He thought, how do I run a practice with fifth graders on a football field? At the coaches meeting, Patrick was attentive. He did not want to let his son down, and, although he was not concerned about winning, he wanted to be prepared. The meeting was informative and Patrick picked up some great drills and ideas for strategy, which eased his anxiety a bit. Nonetheless, Patrick was still worried about how he would connect with the kids and make it a fun environment.

Patrick's Dilemma and Solution

Patrick's hesitancy to coach the flag football team is likely driven by a feeling that he is unprepared as a coach. The situation Patrick finds himself in is common in community youth sport programs. Parents are motived to support their son or daughter's youth sport experience and, sometimes, whether they want to or not, sign up to coach the team. Patrick is approaching his role as a coach to help youth develop sport skills and have fun. He is challenged by his limited knowledge of football and how to effectively work with youth. To fulfill his role as a volunteer community youth sport coach and create an environment focused on fun and effort, Patrick can implement positive and inclusive coaching practices to develop enjoyment, effort, and resilience.

DEVELOPING ENJOYMENT, EFFORT, AND RESILIENCE

For the beginning youth sport coach, three key questions are important to keep in mind: (1) How can I create a fun sport environment? (2) How can I help athletes learn that effort leads to improvement? and (3) How can I help athletes learn from their mistakes? By addressing these three questions coaches can improve athletes' enjoyment, motivation, and resilience. In the end, the team environment is a place where youth and coaches want to be because they are having fun and getting better at their skills. This section looks at how coaches answer these questions.

Creating a Fun Environment

When athletes are asked why they participate in sport, their number-one reason is to have fun.[3] However, many coaches wonder what athletes mean by fun. Sport researchers recently asked youth soccer players to consider what is fun about soccer.[4] While the players described a lot of fun things, here are the top three dimensions of what is fun about soccer:

1. Fun is being on a supportive team where they can connect with one another, feel supported by team members, and play with others that are good sports.
2. Fun is being able to play soccer where they can work hard, be active, and give their best effort.
3. Fun is having a quality coach who knows the sport, praises players, communicates good feedback, and is friendly and respectful.

Their responses provide coaches with many ideas for creating a fun sport environment. This includes providing time for athletes to play the sport and test their skills, encouraging athletes to cheer and help each other, as well as get to know one another, and being friendly and supportive. Additionally, athletes want coaches who know the sport. When coaches know the sport, they can provide athletes variety in practice to keep them active and excited about participating. For example, changing practice drills from day to day, using a variety of activities, and implementing small-sided games. Further, when sport coaches structure practices to help athletes improve their skills and provide quality feedback, it helps them get better.

Reinforcing Effort and Improvement

As noted in the previous section, part of having fun is trying hard and learning new skills. However, it is also important for youth athletes to recognize that their effort makes a difference in their skill development. Coaches can emphasize this mind-set by encouraging self-comparison and providing athletes feedback connecting effort to improvement. While very young athletes may not be able to distinguish between effort and ability,[5] athletes do begin to recognize that some athletes are just better than others because they have more talent and ability. When athletes realize this, they may stop trying, saying they will never be as good as so-and-so. In this case, athletes relinquish their control. However, by turning their focus toward themselves and considering how they can be better than they are now, coaches can help them continue to maintain control and apply effort. Along the way, coaches also help athletes understand what good effort looks like. Here are some examples:

- During a small-sided game, athletes hustle on the field or court rather than walking.
- During a technique drill or learning a new play, athletes are applying mental effort to pick up key cues and memorizing how to do the skill or tactic quickly.
- Outside of practice, athletes devote 10–15 minutes a day to improving a particular skill.
- During conditioning, athletes keep their heart rate in the appropriate heart rate zone.
- Athletes brainstorm with the coach about a new strategy to try to help them improve their skills.

Coaches also want to provide athletes feedback to encourage them to keep trying and, more important, to reinforce the connection that their effort is associated with their improvement. For example, when athletes hustle on the field, a soccer coach could say, "I like the hustle out there! Did you see how when you hustled, you were able to be in the correct position to support your forward. What a great improvement from last time. Keep up the good work!" In another instance, a swim coach might say, "Victoria, that backstroke flip turn is much better. I can see that your 10 minutes of extra practice is really paying off."

CREATING A POSITIVE CLIMATE

The primary goal we stress with our club coaches is that they provide a positive experience that highlights the growth opportunities and life lessons taught through athletic participation. We encourage them to place the values of effort and sportsmanship ahead of winning the game. Another goal is to achieve a balance between competition and fun. If our young athletes don't have fun playing the games, then they're more likely to drop out and less likely to participate in athletics in the future. For us, a positive sport culture exists when there is a high level of engagement from our coaches, athletes, and parents. Kids take their cues from their parents and coaches and they can tell if their adult role models are genuinely motivated and supportive. We're fortunate at our level to have kids that look forward to practices and games each week. Sure, we have a few kids who occasionally admit that their parents signed them up and they'd rather be doing something else on a Saturday morning. That is a challenge all our coaches face. Regardless of the reason youth join our program, we instruct our coaches to make sure that all of kids get an equal amount of playing time. Youth can't develop their athletic abilities and gain confidence if they're on the sidelines. To promote inclusivity at the club, we have a "no cut" policy. Every kid that registers is assigned to a team. In addition, we have a scholarship program that provides financial assistance to parents who may not be able to afford a club membership or sport fees. No kid, regardless of their circumstances, is ever excluded from our athletic programs.

—Scott McClure, athletic director, Boys & Girls Clubs of the Lewis-Clark Valley (ID)

Recognizing the Importance of Learning from Mistakes

Another positive coaching practice is to recognize that mistakes are part of the learning process and that the role of the coach is to help athletes learn from these mistakes rather than yelling, criticizing, or punishing them. In her book, *Mistakes Worth Making*, author Susan Halden-Brown writes that perfection is an unrealistic goal. She notes that a better approach would be to focus on athletic excellence where we accept that mistakes will happen, not let them negatively influence performance, and learn from them.[6] For example, if an athlete serves a tennis ball outside the line, this error should not negatively influence the next serve and a potential double fault. Next, the coach should help the athlete consider how to learn from their mistake and get more tennis balls inside the line by improving physical/mental skills and conditioning. This last part is key, as the only way athletes continue to develop excellence is if they see the error and make improvements. Therefore, the coach's role becomes less about creating a negative vibe around the mistake and telling the athlete not to do it again and more about why the athlete made the mistake and how to help the athlete learn from the mistake. Key questions to consider in helping athletes learn from mistakes are these:

- What is the mistake?
- When does the mistake occur?
- Why does the mistake occur?
- How can the mistake be fixed and when should it be corrected?

Answering these questions helps coaches consider how best to coach the athlete and help the athlete recognize that mistakes and failures provide opportunities for growth. However, it also can reduce the pressure, anxiety, and fear associated with making mistakes, which can lead to further mistakes. In fact, another important strategy coaches can teach to athletes is how to recover from a mistake when it happens in competition. Halden-Brown[7] suggests the following three-step approach to mistake recovery:

1. Recover composure: Do not fall into the trap of thinking more mistakes are coming and become emotionally overwhelmed. Move on from the single mistake because mistakes happen.

2. Refocus: Consider what is controllable and where attention should be focused.
3. Retry: Take advantage of the next opportunity.

This focus on learning and recovering from mistakes also helps athletes to recognize that when faced with mistakes, setbacks, and adversity one does not give up but rather exhibits resilience.

Revisit Scenario 1: Patrick's Dilemma
Based on the content shared here, Patrick has many options. To create a fun environment, Patrick decides to use drills where all the kids can be active and create small-sided games where athletes can test their skills. He will also remind his young players to cheer for each other and will model support by providing a lot of constructive feedback during practices. Patrick also had some great ice breakers that he used when coaching T-ball and he decides to modify these to use with his flag football team. In addition, he would continue his tradition of telling short, one-liner, inoffensive jokes at the start of each practice. Patrick also reaches out to Kylie at Parks and Rec, who shares practice plans and provides some additional resources on teaching techniques. With these resources, Patrick is better prepared to help keep the athletes active and engaged, which will make the experience more enjoyable. To recognize effort, Patrick will make sure his feedback to players acknowledges their effort and shows them how it leads to improvement. At the same time, he will emphasize personal improvement in skills and tactics as the season progresses. Finally, when mistakes are made Patrick will take a moment to consider how best to help the athlete learn from the mistake.

SCENARIO 2: BROOKE THE YOUTH TRAVEL TEAM COACH
The summer heat baked through Brooke's car, even as the AC fan ran on full speed. It was mid-July, and Brooke was staring at the front doors of the gymnasium, hesitant to enter. This was her third summer coaching with the Cottonwood Club Volleyball Program (CCVP). The club paid Brooke a small stipend to coach the U14 team each summer. A former player for the club and a local high school star, Brooke enjoyed the opportunity to share her passion for volleyball with the younger athletes. She also coached the junior varsity team at one of the local high schools.

Like many youth sport clubs, CCVP was a parent-run organization funded mainly through participation fees and a few sponsors. The club had a clear purpose to provide support for a select number of youth sport travel teams in the local community. Because participation opportunities in the club were limited by socioeconomic status, the club had developed the perception that they were exclusive and not open to everyone. From her own experience, this was reality rather than perception. Her hesitancy to enter the gym this afternoon was due to the culture of the club and, more specifically, the climate of her team.

Before the summer tournament season had begun, Brooke, a white coach, recruited a few rising volleyball players from the middle school that fed into the high school where she coached. To build her high school program, she knew she needed to increase the opportunities for young athletes to develop volleyball skills at a younger age. Getting them involved in the club was one option. The enrollment at the high school where she coached included a number of students whose parents were employed as agricultural workers, either in the fruit-packing plants or as farm workers. Many of these families did not have the economic capability to pay the CCVP club fees. Therefore, working with the CCVP and through some fundraising ideas, she was able to get four athletes, who were all from lower socioeconomic backgrounds—three Latina and one white—registered for the summer season. She was excited to help each of these young athletes get more exposure and experience playing with her club team. But, for some reason, her team felt divided. There was an obvious distancing of some of the returning athletes toward the four new athletes. Also, Brooke could tell that all her returning athletes, who were all white and from high socioeconomic backgrounds, were struggling with the new team dynamic. She knew she needed to make some changes to her team climate to make it more welcoming.

Brooke's Dilemma and Solution

In this scenario, Brooke had infused four athletes from different socioeconomic backgrounds and different race/ethnicities into an environment that was homogeneous. Her skills as a coach to create an environment where the four new athletes would feel welcome were being challenged. Because Brooke recognized that she needs to help the new athletes feel more accepted on the team, she already has taken the first step in creating a more welcoming environment. Next, she needs to implement specific strategies to ensure the environment is more inclusive.

Welcoming Everyone to the Team

While developing enjoyment, reinforcing effort, and recognizing the importance of learning from mistakes are essential strategies for coaches to use to create a positive and motivational environment, it is also important to consider how coaches create a welcoming and inclusive environment for athletes. Coaches begin creating a welcoming team by being friendly, kind, and respectful to all athletes (see chapter 4). However, it would be naive to think that welcoming everyone, getting to know them, encouraging a sense of belonging, and honoring their contributions will be enough, something Brooke is beginning to realize.

Sometimes coaches and athletes try to get to know one another, but misunderstandings and disrespect occur due to their differences. Or individuals on the team are unwilling to accept and welcome some people because they are different. These differences can be related to culture, race/ethnicity, gender, sexual orientation, ability, religion, and the list goes on. Therefore, coaches will need to do more to create an inclusive environment. Shawn Ladda[8] offers the six steps of knowing, showing, setting the tone, stepping up and stepping in, following up, and building a legacy for coaches to consider to help all athletes feel welcomed and a part of the team. Here are some ways coaches can use these steps in practice:

1. Knowing: Knowing involves developing knowledge of and attitudes toward various cultures and being willing to learn from others. Coaches develop knowledge in and background of the various cultures and groups represented by team members. Knowing also means coaches reflect upon how their own culture affects them and affects how they interact with other cultures. Further, coaches acknowledge the need to recognize individual differences that exist between people from the same culture.
2. Showing: For example, coaches can role model inclusion by inviting athletes with a disability to be part of the team and provide them accommodations appropriate to the sport environment.

3. Setting the Tone: Coaches can develop team activities that require athletes to understand another person's perspective. This can help athletes learn empathy and listening skills that can reinforce inclusion.

4. Stepping Up and Stepping In: When coaches hear inappropriate language (e.g., don't be sissy, you're crazy), see a racist remark written in the locker room, or observe bullying of a LGBTQIA athlete, they respond swiftly to address the issue and seek to reinforce the team's commitment to a positive and inclusive team environment.

5. Following Up: Coaches should continue to promote inclusion on the team whether it be through team-building activities, reading a book or watching a movie and having a discussion about a topic, or supporting local initiatives important to members of the team.

6. Building a Legacy: Coaches can ask the athletes how they perceive the team climate and how by working together it can be improved, so everyone feels included on the team.

By engaging in these steps, coaches are intentional about their efforts to be inclusive. What it really comes down to is practicing humility. When coaches recognize they have a lot to learn; are willing to listen, learn, and understand; willing to try to see things from another person's point of view; and are respectful, it sets the stage for creating an inclusive team environment.

Revisit Scenario 2: Brooke's Dilemma

Brooke has already begun to employ the six steps by role modeling inclusion and inviting the four athletes to the team. However, she may have an underlying motive for recruiting these players that will need to be addressed. She will also want to learn more about her athletes' backgrounds and the Latinx cultures represented by *Getting to Know* them.

To address the apprehensiveness and potential stereotypes of the other players on the team, Brooke will need to *Set the Tone* of her program, reminding players of the team expectations for interacting with one another and how we welcome all players. Further, Brooke will need to introduce a variety of team-building activities to help the athletes develop trust, comradery, and greater understanding of one another and their cultural and socioeconomic background. There are a variety of team-building activities she could implement, including weekly team meals, a preseason retreat, and community service projects. In addition, she could include daily activities as a part of her practice plan. For example, at the end of practice Brooke could use the "communication circle" to help increase interaction and build relationships among athletes and coaches.[9] In the "communication circle," Brooke has all of the athletes and coaches form a large circle and lock hands. Then she turns to the individual on her right and asks them a question. To build trust among the group, Brooke asks questions that encourage athletes to complement their teammates and share something more personal about themselves. Thus, there is a progression to the type of questions Brooke asks as the season goes on. In other words, early in the season she might request, "Share one thing the teammate to your right did in practice today to make the team better." Later in the season, she might ask, "Share one thing about yourself that we don't know." The communication circle reinforces empathy and humility, which will be important skills to advance for all athletes, but particularly returning athletes. Whether daily, weekly, or once a season, team-building activities are a critical component to creating an environment where everyone feels welcome on the team.

Finally, to *Step Up and In*, Brooke will need to provide stern reminders and/or consequences for those who violate the team expectations. In addition, she will need to have respectful and courageous conversations about race and socioeconomic status and recognize and praise those athletes who are supporting the team expectations.

SCENARIO 3: IAN THE HIGH SCHOOL COACH

Ian glanced up at the clock. "Two more minutes," he blurted. The students hurriedly filled in a couple more multiple choice questions on their American history exam. This was Ian's eighth year teaching American history and coaching track and field at Thornburg High School. He always wanted to be a teacher, and, although he had been an athlete in high school, coaching is something he fell into after securing his first teaching position more than 12 years ago at a nearby middle school. The activities director at the time asked him to serve as a middle school track and field coach. His training as an educator prepared him well in how to create a welcoming environment, thus he was able to make practice fun and provide feedback on effort. However, when it came to providing feedback on the details of athlete performance, he was less effective.

Since he took over as head coach at Thornburg High School, participation numbers for track and field had skyrocketed. Student-athletes enjoyed the positive and welcoming environment he had created around the program and more were signing up each year. But, while participation numbers were high, individual and team performance at the meets were falling short of expectations. Ian knew he needed to do more to help each of them reach their potential.

Ian's Dilemma and Solution

In this scenario, Ian had learned how to coach on the job. While his training as an educator gave him the skills for working with youth and the knowledge of how to create a positive learning environment, he was limited in helping each athlete reach their full potential. To build on the positive and inclusive environment he has already created with his team, Ian could help athletes reach their potential by supporting and nurturing the athlete's mastery of physical, mental, and decision-making skills.

HELPING ATHLETES REACH THEIR POTENTIAL
THROUGH MASTERY, AUTONOMY, AND SUPPORT

As young athletes progress in their sport, they begin to seek ways to further their performance excellence. Within these more intense competitive environments, coaches often wonder how best to motivate, challenge, and enhance the competitive drive of their athletes to achieve athletic excellence. In the process, coaches sometimes lose sight of the positive and inclusive coaching practices. However, having a successful program that is sustainable over time often means integrating athletic excellence with the positive practices. Sport psychology researchers, Joan Duda and her colleagues developed the program Empowering Coaching. The program emphasizes theory-based strategies focused on mastery, autonomy, and support to foster athlete motivation, enjoyment, and well-being, while also advancing athlete development.[10]

Focus on Mastery

Building on recognizing effort and improvement noted earlier in this chapter, coaches interested in building a successful program will want to encourage all athletes on the team to work toward athletic excellence by mastering physical, mental, and critical decision-making skills, continuing to improve conditioning, and masterfully executing game plans. Here are some ideas for coaches to consider:

- Create expectations for excellence. This can occur by developing core values that focus on mastery and excellence and creating standards of performance (see chapter 2) to help guide practice planning as well as athlete attentional focus and effort on achieving the standards.
- Use goal setting. Have athletes set goals that align with the standards of performance. By having individual meetings with team members, coaches can help athletes set individual goals that will further their own development and support the team's performance. Throughout the season, the coach can then evaluate their goal achievement and help each athlete see how they are contributing to team success.
- Reinforce the connection between effort and improvement. For example, a coach could assess athletes early in the season on conditioning or skills and then reassess at various times throughout the season showing them their improvement and discuss how their effort during training sessions has continued to help them get better. The key is for athletes to recognize that what they do in practice matters for how they will perform in competition.

Encourage Autonomy

Helping athletes achieve performance excellence also requires providing athletes the opportunity to play a role in their own training and development. Coaches often speak of wanting athletes to be more accountable, however, many training environments are set up with the coach telling the athlete what to do, where to be, when to do it, and how to do it. In many ways, practices strip athletes of ownership over their own development. Therefore, coaches should consider ways they can help athletes participate in their own development. Sport researchers, Geneviève Mageau and Robert Vallerand, offer the following suggestions:[11]

- Provide athletes choice. Coaches can consider whether there are aspects of practices where athletes can make choices. For example, could middle school athletes be provided guided choices about warm-ups and cooldown? Could high school athletes be provided different training sets that accomplish the same goal and let athletes choose? Could athletes decide what events to compete in at the next competition or who the starters should be for the next game?

- Afford athletes the opportunity to participate. When athletes have been part of a program for a while they begin to understand the why and how of daily practices, particularly if coaches are transparent about their plans. Therefore, coaches could consider giving veteran athletes opportunities to construct practices based on the daily practice goals. At the end of practice, coaches may also ask athletes what they still need to work on to be a better athlete or team. The coach could then use their feedback to create the practice plan for the next day.

- Encourage athlete decision making. Coaches can help to improve ownership by providing opportunities in practices and games for young athletes to make their own decisions and reflect on those decisions. By encouraging athletes to think about the what, where, why, and how in game situations, coaches can improve tactical decision making. As athletes improve in their abilities to do this, coaches can begin to turn some of this decision-making power over to athletes, helping them to take ownership of play on the field or court.

The important thing to consider in developing autonomy is that coaches need to prepare athletes to take ownership of their own development. Coaches do this by educating athletes about the sport and training principles and providing them guided feedback so they can make decisions that support their own and the team's path toward excellence.

Support Development

Another key element is for coaches to care enough to support all athletes in developing excellence. This support takes many forms including the following:

- Consider athletes' needs. When coaches get to know each athlete on the team, they can create practices that will meet their needs and align with their interests. By doing so, coaches demonstrate their interest in their development. Additionally, coaches who know an athlete needs to work on a particular skill can provide time after practice or resources to help the athlete get better.

- Provide useful information. Coaches provide all sorts of information to athletes that can support development, including providing quality feedback for all athletes to help them improve and educating athletes on various aspects of the sport.
- Encourage athletes. Coaches also support athletes by looking for opportunities to provide well-meaning praise during practice, encouraging athletes when they encounter setbacks or adversity in practices or competition, and being a sounding board when they experience struggles.

Revisit Scenario 3: Ian's Dilemma

Ian, in learning this information, realizes that while he has a good grasp of creating a welcoming environment, he is not able to help his track and field athletes reach their full potential through autonomy, mastery, and support. Therefore, for next season, Ian decides he is going to initiate a goal-setting program with the athletes. He will meet with the group to describe the goal-setting process for the season and have individual meetings with athletes to identify goals for the end of season. Then, using short-term goals along the way, he will incorporate strategies in practice to achieve the long-term goals. Throughout the season, Ian will remind the athletes of their goals to show them their improvement and the importance of their effort. Additionally, he will tell them how the goal strategies are being incorporated into daily practice (i.e., providing a rationale for training), and after events, he will ask each athlete to come by to debrief about the race/event. During this meeting they can work together to highlight what went well and what can be incorporated into their practices in the coming weeks to foster further improvement. Using this process, Ian will be building his athletes' decision-making skills and providing opportunities to help them be accountable for their own training. By engaging in the goal-setting process, Ian also supports his athletes by constructing practices around their goals (i.e., accommodating their needs and interests) and providing important feedback and encouragement to achieve their goals.

CREATING A SUPPORTIVE SETTING FOR ATHLETE GROWTH

Over the past 25 years of coaching gymnasts, I have been fortunate to see the benefits of being involved in a gymnastics program. As a team coach, I have the opportunity to start working with gymnasts as early as six years old and often remain their coach until they graduate. Gymnastics is, at its core, a sport of falling and getting back up, and we take great pride in teaching our gymnasts tips, tricks, and the courage of how to get back up after each fall. But just like in life our gymnasts learn to understand it is not the failure that defines you but what you do after it. After an athlete fails, I discuss what happened, how we can learn from the mistake, and what tools are needed to get them up and make another attempt, to move forward. Gymnasts move at different speeds and at different ages through the levels. This movement helps in creating and perpetuating a fun and safe environment where learning and succeeding is possible. Since our program has teams of all ages, our younger gymnasts are mentored by older gymnasts; they look up to them, aspiring to be like them, and desire to one day transform themselves into a mentor for the next generation. I find through coach instruction and our mentor system we are able to better support our gymnasts and open up the door for greater potential. In gymnastics it is very common to practice anywhere from 6 to 20 hours a week. In order to balance these hours, prevent injuries and burnout, fun is the tool used to keep our gymnasts training hard. We use games, peer competitions, and positive reinforcement in all our coaching to get the very best results out of our athletes. Throughout this time, inevitably there are moments where gymnasts struggle and begin to doubt themselves and their abilities. When this occurs, I have an individual conversation with them about how it is OK to struggle and how hard work can and will pay off. We talk about how often in life, some of the greatest triumphs come from the hardest efforts. I tell them to trust in their training, do the best they can that day, and to believe in themselves because their coaches do.

—Josh Burnham, team director/coach/owner,
Lone Mountain Gymnastics (MT)

CONCLUSION

All coaches want to create a sports environment where their youth athletes are excited to be, improve their skills, develop a passion for the sport, build friendships, and feel like part of a team. This chapter gives a starting point for creating such an environment by providing coaches strategies that emphasize fun, effort, resilience, belonging, inclusiveness, improvement, ownership, and support. Coaches are encouraged to implement positive and inclusive coaching practices in their own sport setting and, over time, create team traditions that carry over to the next group of athletes.

COACH TIPS!

- Reflect on daily coaching practice to ensure you are providing a fun setting.
- Reinforce effort and how it leads to improvement.
- Help athletes learn from mistakes by creating an environment where they feel it is safe to make them.
- Communicate a sense of belonging among members of the team.
- Set the tone by role modeling empathy and reinforcing inclusive practices.
- Develop team-building activities to reinforce the team culture.
- Consider ways to develop cultural humility by learning about other cultures and recognizing how one's own culture influences interactions with others.
- Help athletes reach their potential through mastery, autonomy, and support.

COACH DEVELOPER TIPS!

- Observe the coach's ability to reinforce effort and help athletes learn from mistakes.
- Provide resources to assist coaches in establishing inclusive practices.
- Assist the coach by providing feedback on how the coach's team climate aligns with the overall climate of the sport organization.
- Establish a climate within the sport organization that supports coaches reflecting on how their own culture and behaviors influence their interactions with others.

6

To Coach Is to
Keep Athletes Safe

Youth sport provides athletes an environment where they can develop sport skills, build friendships with their peers, and try a new sport for the first time. Achieving these outcomes also requires coaches to keep young athletes in the game by providing them a safe place to learn and participate. Youth sport coaches take a variety of actions to ensure a safe environment for the athletes under their watch. For example, a youth soccer coach will remove a fallen tree limb from the soccer pitch after a recent storm; a youth sport camp coach will make a water cooler available for participants during their summer sport camp; a middle school volleyball coach will require athletes and parents to sign a code of conduct prior to the start of the season; and a private sport gymnastics coach will have parents and athletes watch a video on the potential risks and injuries associated with the sport of gymnastics, then have both sign a waiver indicating they understand their risks. In each of these examples the coach is taking steps to provide an environment for safe sport participation. However, in each of these examples coaches will want to consider the following:

- Does the youth soccer coach inspect the field daily for potential flaws and changes to the playing surface?
- Does the summer camp coach know how to recognize the signs of heat-related illness in athletes and how often to provide water breaks based on the current heat conditions?

- Does the volleyball coach utilize the code of conduct to minimize potential hazing and bullying behavior?
- Does the gymnastics coach know how to recognize when an athlete might be predisposed to an injury and understand how to modify practice procedures to reduce injury risks and utilize proper periodization methods to ensure safe progression of physical training programs?

To ensure the setting is physically and emotionally safe to keep athletes in the game, coaches will want to engage in careful planning to create a safe environment and use safe training practices.

CREATING A SAFE ENVIRONMENT

Part of keeping athletes in the game is creating a psychologically and emotionally safe environment. While this begins with creating a positive and inclusive culture, as described in chapter 5, it also entails making sure the setting is free of harassment as well as physical and emotional abuse. Therefore, coaches need to be able to recognize harassment and abuse, establish a respectful environment and manage the environment so it remains respectful and free of harassment and abuse.

Recognizing Harassment and Abuse

In order for coaches to address harassment and abuse when it happens, they must first recognize it. Table 6.1 provides definitions of each of these terms along with potential warning signs. By understanding key terms, the coach has a foundation to ensure they are establishing and managing a respectful environment. However, all coaches are encouraged to complete a SafeSport Training Course as mandated by law and their sport organizations to learn more about how to recognize harassment and abuse (see appendix).

Establishing a Respectful Environment

Coaches recognize that their role in keeping athletes in the game will go beyond just identifying these behaviors. Coaches need to establish environments that reduce the likelihood of this behavior, address issues as they occur, and report behaviors to appropriate authorities. Coaches can establish a respectful environment by making respect and kindness part of the core values of the sport program, which will then be discussed, modeled, and practiced throughout the season. Here are a few ideas:

Table 6.1. Key Terms for Recognizing Harassment and Abuse

Term	Definition	Examples
Harassment	"Harassment is unwelcome conduct that is based on race, color, religion, sex (including pregnancy), national origin, age (40 or older), disability or genetic information."[1]	Offensive jokes Intimidation Name calling Insults
Physical abuse	"Any non-accidental physical harm inflicted by a person responsible for a child's care that may or may not cause physical injury to that child."[2]	Hitting/slapping Throwing objects at Shaking
Emotional abuse	"A pattern of deliberate non-contact behaviors by a person within a critical relationship role that has the potential to be harmful. Acts of emotional abuse include physical behaviors, verbal behaviors, and acts of denying attention and support."[3]	Creating fear Denying emotional responses Publicly rejecting someone Exploiting someone for own benefit
Sexual abuse	"While the legal definition of child sexual abuse varies from state to state, sexual abuse is commonly defined as sexual exploitation involving anal, genital, oral, or breast contact between a child and another person and/or exposing a child to language or images of a sexual nature."[4]	Engaging in sexual acts Exposing individuals to sexual images or language Touching someone's genitals, breast, etc.
Bullying	Bullying is repeated (or potential to be repeated) aggressive behavior designed to hurt another that involves a power imbalance.[5]	Teasing Threatening harm Physically hurting someone Spreading rumors Pranking someone's phone
Hazing	"Any potentially humiliating, degrading, abusive, or dangerous activity expected of a junior-ranking athlete by a more senior teammate, which does not contribute to either athlete's positive development, but is required to be accepted as part of a team, regardless of the junior-ranking athlete's willingness to participate. This includes, but is not limited to, any activity, no matter how traditional or seemingly benign, that sets apart or alienates any teammate based on class, number of years on the team, or athletic ability."[6]	Forced activities on junior-ranking athletes to prove worth Humiliation of junior-ranking athletes Beating or isolating new members

Sources:
1. "Harassment," U.S. Equal Employment Opportunity Commission, accessed September 21, 2020, https://www.eeoc.gov/harassment.
2. *Parent Toolkit* (U.S. Center for Safe Sport), 8.
3. Ashley E. Stirling and Gretchen A. Kerr, "Defining and Categorizing Emotional Abuse in Sport," *European Journal of Sport Science* 8, no. 4 (2008): 178, doi:10.1080/17461390802086281.
4. *Parent Toolkit*, 6.
5. Peter K. Smith, "Bullying: Definition, Types, Causes, Consequences and Intervention," *Social and Personality Psychology Compass* 10, no. 9 (2016): 519, doi:10.1111/spc3.12266.
6. R. Brian Crow and Eric W. Macintosh, "Conceptualizing a Meaningful Definition of Hazing in Sport," *European Sport Management Quarterly* 9, no. 4 (2009): 433–51. https://doi.org/10.1080/16184740903331937.

- Open discussion: Coaches can have a brief discussion about bullying and share resources during a practice (see appendix).
- Code of conduct: Coaches can develop a code of conduct around respectful behaviors that include a list of consequences for infractions. The code of conduct can be shared during the first team meeting and include a discussion about what respectful behaviors look like and how to avoid disrespectful behaviors. For example, learning to control one's emotions may be key for avoiding disrespectful behaviors.
- Team traditions: Another strategy coaches can implement is developing team traditions and team-building activities that encourage connection rather than hazing. For example, having team dinners, engaging in community service together as a team, and developing a big sister/little sister program all send the message that being initiated into the team means helping new athletes feel a part of the team. In turn, team traditions can assist the coach in teaching and reinforcing the core values of the program.[1] In addition, by encouraging team captains or veteran athletes to organize these events, they gain leadership experience and engage in positive behaviors on behalf of the team.
- Positive and inclusive practice: Finally, coaches are encouraged to engage in positive and inclusive cultural practices (see chapters 4 and 5), like focusing on encouragement, praise, and support, rather than guilt or shame. It will be important throughout this process for coaches to reflect on how athletes are responding to their behaviors and whether it is promoting a respectful and harassment-free environment or not.

IN ACTION

STRATEGIES FOR HELPING ATHLETES
FEEL SUPPORTED AND SAFE

As a female collegiate athlete on the men's team during the creation and implementation of Title IX, and the first woman inducted into Whittier College Athletic Hall of Fame, I know how important a positive and safe environment is to an athlete. It starts with knowing your players as a whole person and creating a team culture that values every player on the team. I have coached the Corvallis High School Girls Tennis Team to five straight Oregon State 5A championships in five years. Prior to our title run, we invested a significant amount of time into getting to know each athlete, on and off the court. We implemented communication-style reflections, required daily journal entries, written coach feedback, and a tie-dye party. Each of these was just as crucial to our success as drills and skill development. Also, we used a coach and team captain guided team-within-a-team point system to create a "As One" team philosophy. My adapted "As One" team philosophy, borrowed from Jackson Vaughan at Linfield College, allows *all* team members to find a safe and supported place on the team, no matter their skill level or background. It takes work to be a coach, no matter what level. It's a lot of work to create a positive team culture. It is an even greater amount of work to combine positive team culture with your love and knowledge of your sport and have a winning season. If you are a coach looking for a way to create a positive and safe team environment, start with relationships, trust, and shared experiences, and your players will be happy and unstoppable.

—Donna Keim, head girls' tennis coach/teacher,
Corvallis High School, College Hill, OR

IN ACTION

TRAINING COACHES TO PROVIDE A SAFE ENVIRONMENT

As a youth sports administrator, our mission at Eagle Parks and Recreation is to provide a fun, nonintimidating setting for our youth to learn and grow in a team sports environment. The foundation of our mission lies within the training of our volunteer

(*continued*)

TRAINING COACHES TO PROVIDE
A SAFE ENVIRONMENT (*continued*)

coaches. We train our volunteer coaches with the intent that they will have a positive impact on kids' lives and provide a memorable experience for all athletes. During our annual coaches meeting, we provide volunteer coaches a foundation in general coaching principles that includes sportsmanship, fundamental skills, teamwork, and responsibility. In addition, we provide information on how to communicate with parents, strategies on how to organize a practice, and tips on how to work with young athletes. Our mission coupled with our approach to training volunteer coaches is vital in making our youth programs a success and to ensure our athletes will have a positive learning experience.

—Brandon "Beeg" Johnson, Parks and Recreation director,
Eagle Parks and Recreation, Eagle, ID

Managing a Respectful Environment

The next step coaches can take is to manage the environment so it remains free of harassment or abuse. This means recognizing and addressing harassment, abuse, bullying, and hazing, as well as reporting it. Addressing inappropriate behavior begins with immediately investigating the actions of an athlete. Then discussing the behavior with the offender so the athlete understands why the behavior is wrong, how it has an impact on others, and how to reduce the likelihood of it occurring in the future. Finally, coaches need to impose a consequence for the athlete's behavior. Coaches may also want to consider training their athletes to recognize and respond to such behavior by having them participate in bystander interventions. *Bystander Revolution*[2] provides examples of how individuals can intervene when bullying and hazing occurs (see appendix). However, coaches also need to consider what reporting is required by law within their state or district, as well as regulations within their organization. Many organizations have guidelines for reporting bullying and hazing acts and many states have requirements for reporting abuse (see resources in the appendix to determine your legal obligations as a youth sport coach). In the following short story, consider which of the above strategies Walt might want to employ to mitigate a bullying-type behavior in the weight room.

WALT, THE WRESTLING COACH

In his third year as the head wrestling coach at Central High School, Walt was looking forward to the upcoming wrestling season. He had potential state champion wrestlers in three different weight classes and this team was committed to improving themselves on the mat, as evident by the time they had spent in the weight room during the offseason. Central High School was a new midsize high school that served the suburban growth of the regional metropolitan area. The school district was well funded by local taxpayers and equipped with a first-class weight room.

There was a strength and conditioning class taught by one of the physical education teachers who was certified in strength and conditioning. However, her duties were to the general student population and not athletics. Nonetheless, she liked to help coaches, like Walt, design training programs for their athletes. With her assistance, Walt designed a program specifically for his athletes to use in the offseason and preseason. The program allowed his athletes to participate in the conditioning program while competing in other sports, and a majority of the wrestlers did so.

Due to the time constraints of also serving as a mathematics teacher and as an assistant coach with the football team, Walt did not supervise the weight room when his athletes were working out. Central High School had established a weight room supervisor position, which was often filled by an assistant coach for an extra stipend. In this case, the supervisor was a young college student, serving as a volunteer basketball coach. He had limited knowledge of strength and conditioning, and his main responsibility was to ensure the facility was clean, picked up, and athletes were not engaging in horseplay. The school set aside time for each team to use the facility as well as open lifting time for all high school students.

During one of the scheduled training sessions for wrestlers, two junior wrestlers approached a couple of the incoming wrestlers while one of the athletes was finishing a set of dumbbell presses, with the other one spotting.

"How much weight are you lifting, weenie," quipped one of the juniors, while flexing his pecs in the direction of two freshman. "Have you hit puberty yet?"

Both the juniors laughed. The second junior piped up, "Let me show you how it is done, wimps."

He grabbed two 75-pound dumbbells and ripped out 5 reps, then let the dumbbells drop by his feet, reverberating a large thud across the weight room. The junior got up, posturing, and said, "That's how it is done, wuss." Then he reached out and grabbed one of the athlete's pectoral muscles. "No wonder, there is nothing here," he stated, looking at the other junior. They both laughed and walked away.

Questions to Consider
1. How is the interaction an act of bullying?
2. What impact might this type of behavior have on the first-year athletes and their participation in the wrestling program?
3. What type of strategies could Walt employ to ensure the weight room is a safe and respectful environment for all athletes in the program, even if he is not present?

Walt's Role and Responsibility
In this scenario, it is unlikely Walt would be aware of the behavior of his upper-class athletes. However, he should know that athletes may engage in bullying behavior. If Walt were to employ each of the strategies for establishing and managing a respectful environment previously mentioned he could mitigate this type of behavior. Listed below are some ideas:

1. Clear expectations: In a preseason meeting with his team and during the parent meeting, Walt could outline the code of conduct for his program. The code of conduct could address bullying- and hazing-type behavior, emphasizing its application to offseason and preseason programs. In practice sessions throughout the season, Walt could bring up the topic and readdress his expectations, even generating a Q&A session to allow his athletes to discuss the topic in more detail.
2. Establish team traditions: Walt could implement a team tradition that encourages welcoming new athletes to the team. For example, at the beginning of each season the junior and seniors could host a welcoming team dinner where they cook and serve the meal. During the dinner, the juniors

and seniors could show video highlights from the past season and talk about what it meant to be a member of this team.

3. Positive and inclusion practices: As a coach, Walt needs to create and role model an environment that focuses on encouragement and support. For example, if the athletes observe their coach praising other athletes, teaching to correct mistakes, and providing support when they need motivation, the culture of the program is more likely to support these types of behaviors, even when the coach is not present.

USING SAFE TRAINING PRACTICES

Another part of keeping athletes in the game is reducing their risk of physical injury. To ensure the physical safety of athletes during practice, the youth sport coach will want to be aware of proper training principles; monitor the safety of equipment, facilities, and the environment; and consider the role of hydration and nutrition during training.[3]

Reducing Injury Risk with Proper Training Principles

While it is not expected that a youth sport coach be certified as an athletic trainer or be an expert in sport injury and prevention, youth coaches need to consider the following principles prior to and when working with youth athletes:

- Review all athletes' health forms to be aware of any preexisting conditions that could be influenced by participation in exercise (e.g., exercise-induced asthma, diabetes, previous athletic injury, female athlete triad). Once identified, coaches can make further adjustments for individualized training. Additionally, if an athlete has had an injury, coaches will want to have written documentation from a medical professional providing permission to return to play, along with return-to-play guidelines to follow during practice.
- Identify best practices for warming up and cooling down athletes to prevent the risk of injury during practice sessions.
- Supervise the practice session to avoid incorrect practice procedures or potential horseplay.
- Follow appropriate training principles (e.g., overload, progression, specificity) when training athletes (see chapter 7).

- Assess each athlete's fitness levels to make sure all athletes have the appropriate level of physical conditioning to engage in particular activities. If not, consider ways to develop physical conditioning to reduce the risk of injury.
- Monitor athletes to make sure they are not participating in too much training, which can result in overtraining, increasing exhaustion, and risk of injury.
- Plan practices to provide appropriate progression of skill development to reduce risk resulting from lack of expertise in the skill.

For the youth coach seeking additional or more detailed information on this topic, see the resources listed in the appendix.

Reducing Injury with Safety Checks

Another way for coaches to reduce the risk of physical injury in their sport practices is to consider regular safety checks. Administrators and coaches should regularly inspect the facility to make sure it is free of hazards, complies with national sport organization guidelines for use with the particular age level, and is accessible to emergency medical personnel in the case of an emergency. Equipment should also be reviewed to make sure it aligns with the appropriate guidelines for sport safety. Finally, administrators should make coaches aware of appropriate guidelines for practicing under a variety of environmental conditions related to heat (see appendix).

Reducing Injury and Supporting Development with Appropriate Hydration and Nutrition

Appropriate hydration and nutritional practices can promote athlete performance, reduce the risk of injury, and continue to foster appropriate growth and maturation during key developmental periods.[4,5] While coaches should not be providing nutritional advice to athletes on how to lose or gain weight without the guidance of a registered sport dietician, coaches do need to help their athletes stay hydrated during practices and competitions as well as encourage nutritional practices that will help athletes replenish energy stores and promote recovery between exercise events. Therefore, coaches want to be aware of hydration recommendations during and after practice and how to help athletes determine whether they are dehydrated.[6] Additionally, coaches want to encourage athletes to eat healthy foods during the season that support the level of training they are engaged in during that season.[7] Coaches who are interested in more detailed information regarding carbohydrate and protein recommendations for recovery and dietary supplements and nutritional ergogenic aids are encouraged to review the Sports Dietitians Australia Position Statement on sports nutrition for the adolescent athlete.[8]

Responding to Injuries

In case of injuries happening on the field, coaches also want to be aware of appropriate protocols in an emergency situation. Therefore, coaches should be aware of their organization's emergency action plan and understand their role in the process (see appendix). Additionally, coaches will want to know their state and local requirements for coach training requirements in first aid, cardiopulmonary resuscitation, and concussion management. The responsibility for attending to injuries will vary based on the youth sport setting in. In some venues, youth sport administrators will attend to injuries; in other venues, sports medicine professionals care for injuries; and other times the responsibility for injury care falls to the coach. Whether it is required or not, at a minimum, all youth sport coaches should be trained in first aid, CPR/AED, and concussion protocol.

Hopefully, this overview of safe training practices provides coaches with ideas for reducing injury and encourages them to seek out more information. To further help coaches support safety and reduce the risk of injury, the National Athletic Training Association and the North American Booster Club Association created a checklist to help remind coaches, administrators, and parents of their role in creating a safe sport training environment (see appendix for a link to the checklist).

MARTA, THE SOCCER COACH

Marta is a first-year U10 soccer coach but has been around soccer all of her life. Prior to the start of the season she completed the required coach education course and is aware of her responsibilities regarding safety on the field. Therefore, she decides to implement a variety of safety training protocols for the upcoming season, including the following:

1. Prior to the start of the season she reviews all of the athletes' medical forms to determine if there are any underlying health issues she should

be aware of during practice sessions. She discovers one of her athletes has type 1 diabetes and contacts the parents to learn more about the severity of the medical condition and the recommended protocol for when the athlete is engaged in exercise. She learns this is the first athletic experience for the child and the parents are not sure what to expect. However, in consultation with their doctor they have developed a diabetes care plan based on recommendations from the National Athletic Trainers' Association's Position Statement.[9] The position statement describes preexercise and postexercise procedures related to food intake and monitoring blood sugar levels as well as symptoms for Marta to watch out for during practice. The parents also offer to attend every practice and competition to help implement the plan. Marta is appreciative of the information and assistance. She tells the parents she will share this plan with her youth sport administrator who will be serving as the safety officer during practices and competitions as well as encourages them to attend practices and games.

2. Given that this is Marta's first year coaching, she is not really sure where to start with planning practices. Fortunately, her administrator shares with her progressive plans developed by another soccer program.[10] She decides to implement these plans. She also introduces a brief team warm-up and cool-down to provide her an opportunity to connect with players, share announcements, and provide concluding feedback.

3. Marta decides to print out her updated practice plan and add a few additional safety notes. Her first safety note is to arrive a little early to the outdoor practice facility to do a quick field check prior to practice. Her second safety note includes times during practice when she will encourage her athletes to take a quick water break. Based on guidelines from Heather Mangieri (2018), Marta builds in two water breaks 20 and 40 minutes into the practice to have athletes drink 3 to 5 ounces of water.[11] Her final safety note is to have them hydrate at the end of practice and then have them eat a quick, healthy snack brought by a parent that meets the appropriate ratio of carbohydrates to proteins.

CONCLUSION

While it is unrealistic to expect a youth sport coach to have the requisite knowledge in all the areas relative to providing a safe environment in youth sport, it is important that a coach working in youth sport be aware of each of these topics and where to seek additional resources relative to the context they work in. Further, sport administrators will want to be well versed in safety concerns providing support and resources to their youth sport coaches as well as athletes and their families. Overall, creating a safe environment and using safe training practices is a collective responsibility and requires the diligent and concerted efforts of the sport administrator, first and foremost, with youth sport coaches taking appropriate and informed action.

COACH TIPS!
- Learn to recognize situations that may lead to harassment and abuse.
- Complete a SafeSport Training Course.
- Develop a code of conduct to set clear expectations for the team and reinforce respectful behavior.
- Learn proper training principles to reduce injury risk.
- Implement safety checks as part of your daily practice routine.
- Add hydration breaks appropriate to the environment and focus on nutrition for recovery.
- Become first aid and CPR certified.

COACH DEVELOPER TIPS!
- Establish a code of conduct for all sport programs under your guidance.
- Provide training, in-house or outsourced, for coaches on best practices in regard to creating a safe sport environment and using safe training practices.
- Assist coaches in locating and accessing resources on creating a safe sport environment.
- Develop emergency action plans and facility/equipment checklists for coaches to use within the organization.
- Review and discuss practice plans with coaches to determine if they are following safe training practices.
- Evaluate the coaches progress through feedback and annual evaluations to ensure safe sport practices are being implemented.

7

To Coach Is to Plan

The ability of the coach to properly prepare is one of the key indicators of their long-term success and ability to provide a quality sport experience for youth athletes while promoting their development. The first step in proper preparation for coaches is to identify the key areas where coaches plan and then to determine the outcomes they are striving to reach in each area. These areas include planning progression in athlete development, designing conditioning programs, mapping out competitive strategies for the season, and creating mental and life-skill training programs.

PROPER PREPARATION: THE CASE OF THE SWIM COACH

Brianna's toes curled over the edge of the pool deck; her heels raised slightly. Her body teetered out toward the water like she was getting ready to jump in. But her posture was based on her intense focus on two of her competitive swimmers as they finished a timed training lap. This past week, Brianna had developed and implemented a training program to improve their speed. This was a test, and she was hoping the program had worked. Brianna was in the middle of her third season with the Sharks Swim Club team, a community club swimming program for youth ages 6 to 18.

The Sharks Swim Club offers swim lessons and a competitive swim team for all ages. The club paid Brianna an annual stipend to manage the year-round instructional program and serve as the head coach for the U11–U14 competitive summer swim teams. Her duties included hiring swim instructors for the swim lessons, scheduling pool time, supervising volunteer assistant coaches, hosting swim meets, and planning training sessions for all the athletes in the program.

Brianna grew up around the pool. She swam competitively on a swim team and spent four years as a lifeguard during college. After earning her business management degree and completing a local internship with the city pool, she was hired as the assistant manager of the local city swim center and started volunteering as an assistant coach with the Sharks Swim Club. Three years later she was promoted to manager of the swim center and a year later she became the head coach and manager of the Sharks Swim Club. She loved coaching, and during her four years as an assistant, she would spend all her free time learning about training methods, motivational strategies, and how to teach swimming techniques. She would get most of her information from other swim coaches, online videos, and a few coaching clinics she attended. While she was hungry for information and was learning a lot, she did not necessarily know how to implement everything she was learning in her role as a coach. For example, she knew she needed to be careful not to overtrain her athletes, but how was she supposed to set up a training program to avoid this and still challenge them to get better?

Furthermore, while Brianna was passionate about coaching, her management roles took quite a bit of her time. One minute she might be coordinating with the city maintenance department about a recent temperature drop in the pool water and the next adjusting the schedule for a lifeguard that called in sick. In between all of this, usually at lunch, she would plan the daily practice for the swim team. After practice, she would hurry back to her office and check on the next round of lifeguards, respond to messages from community members about swimming programs, and get the pool ready for evening swim lessons. All of her daily responsibilities did not give her much time to reflect on how the practice session went that day, and, given her limited background in best coaching practices, she did not know where to begin to improve her ability to plan for coaching her athletes.

THE IMPORTANCE OF PROPER PLANNING

Legendary and hall of fame basketball coach John Wooden often stated, "Failing to prepare is preparing to fail."[1] Although he did not coin the phrase,

Coach Wooden believed that one of the keys to reaching competitive great-ness is making sure you are prepared. One way coaches can be prepared is to make sure they make time for proper preparation. Proper preparation involves not only making time to plan but also having the competence to know what you are planning for. For example, in the scenario, Brianna is stressed for time and has limited knowledge about how best to plan training programs for her athletes across all age levels, both of which impact her ability to adequately plan for daily practices and make adjustments along the way. To help her overcome her limited training as a coach, while working within the constraints of her daily schedule, Brianna can implement planning. This begins with planning for the long-term development of her athletes and even-tually leading to more specific planning in relation to physical conditioning, competitive strategy, and mental and life-skill preparation.

PLANNING FOR LONG-TERM DEVELOPMENT IN SPORT

To begin the planning process, youth sport coaches want to create plans to support their athletes' developmental pathway in the sport. For example, how coaches plan to work with 8-year-olds will differ compared to how they will plan to work with 15-year-olds in terms of holistic development goals, skills and training methods, and competition schedules. The long-term develop-ment framework can provide coaches the guidance they need. Long-term development is the idea that coaches consider the developmental pathway of athletes over time, which not only guides how they train and develop athletes but also, and more important, prepares them to be active for life by develop-ing their physical literacy.[2,3] To help coaches plan for implementing principles of long-term development to promote physical literacy in their own coaching practice, the following key concepts are recommended by Istvan Bayli and colleagues[4] as well as by Canada's Sport for Life's *Long-Term Development in Sport and Physical Activity* framework.[5]

1. *Focus on Physical Literacy.* "Physical literacy can be described as the motivation, confidence, physical competence, knowledge and under-standing to value and take responsibility for engagement in physical activities for life."[6] While acquiring physical literacy occurs across one's lifetime, youth sport coaches can help athletes become physically literate by assessing and teaching fundamental movement skills (e.g., running,

throwing, kicking) and teaching athletes about the rules, techniques, and tactics of their sport. These actions help athletes develop their physical competence (their ability to do the skill), their confidence in completing the skill, and their knowledge of the sport and how to participate. By having knowledge, competency, and confidence, athletes should be more likely to participate (motivation) and have greater appreciation and enjoyment of the sport (understanding). However, motivation and understanding does not only depend upon having knowledge, competency, and confidence, it also depends on whether the coach created a positive and enjoyable sports environment.

2. *Use Developmentally Appropriate Spaces, Equipment, and Competitive Structures.* Equipment, facilities, and activities should match the structure and stature of athletes. For example, a nine-year-old athlete playing basketball should have a ball that fits the structure of the hand and a basket height that matches his or her stature. Additionally, activities are organized to allow for optimal challenge; that is, an activity or drill allows for individual variation in structure and stature as well as ability. Further, athletes are matched based on stature and structure in competitive situations. Finally, coaches recognize some youth develop more quickly than others (early versus late maturers). Given the difficulty in determining the growth and maturation of any athlete, it is important for youth coaches to emphasize individual athlete improvement rather than competitive outcomes. Competitive outcomes may just be the result of the accelerated height and weight of a young athlete. If an early-maturing athlete relies on this difference and does not work on technical and tactical skills, when the late-maturing athletes catch up in size, the early-maturing athlete will lag behind in skills. This may lead the early-maturing athlete to leave the sport due to a lack of success. The reverse can be true for the late maturer during the early years.

3. *Plan Season or Program Based on Athlete Developmental Pathway.* Coaches want to consider where their athletes are in their growth and development journey as this will determine structure of practice, types of skills and conditioning, amount of training, and key concepts to introduce. Table 7.1 provides some considerations for coaches in planning to work with athletes at varying developmental stages. Table 7.1 is adapted from the *Long-Term Development in Sport and Physical Activity* framework[7] and

Table 7.1. Plan Season on Athlete Developmental Pathway

Age	Structure of Practice	Skills Taught	Type of Conditioning	Key Concepts	Amount of Training
6–8 years of age	• Free play (50%) • Adult-led (structured) play (35%) • Adult instruction (15%)	• Fundamental movement skills • Basic life skills (e.g., respect and self-control)	• Balance • Coordination • Agility • Speed • Flexibility	• Rules and etiquette of the sport	• Encourage participating in multiple activities with small percentage of time spent in sport-related activities (~25%)
Pre-adolescents	• Training (70%) • Competition-specific training and competitions (30%)—playing a variety of positions on team sports	• Fundamental movement skills • Technical and tactical skills • Mental skills • Life skills	• Balance • Coordination • Agility • Speed • Flexibility • Strength	• Basic training structure (i.e., warm-up, cool-down) • Hydration • Fair play	• Sport-specific training 3 times a week • Participation in multiple sports throughout the year
Adolescents	• Training (40%) • Competition-specific training and competitions (60%)	• Technical and tactical skill refinements • Mental skills • Life skills	• Endurance • Strength • Speed • Power • Balance • Coordination • Agility • Flexibility	• Key training principles • Importance of sleep and nutrition for recovery • Ethical sport participation (fair play, clean sport)	• Sport-specific training 6–9 times a week across all sport activities • More time spent in primary sport but still multisport participation

informed by Bayli and colleagues.[8] In reviewing the table, coaches can see that if they were coaching eight-and-under soccer athletes that the emphasis would include some initial balance and coordination activities for warm-up, followed by a few fun small-sided, self-competing, and cooperative games that are structured to improve fundamental movement skills (e.g., running and kicking), while keeping the athletes active. As adolescent athletes progress from pre-adolescence through adolescence into high school, the focus would be on more individualized training of technical and tactical skills and conditioning based on testing and performance, as well as more time on mental skills training.

4. *Create a Progression of Development within the Sport Season.* Youth coaches will want to progressively teach technical and tactical skills over the course of the season. For example, a seven-year-old athlete participating in soccer would first need to be able to run and kick before a coach would consider teaching dribbling and passing. Therefore, during the sport season, coaches should plan a progression of skills that begin with fundamental movements and then progressively teach sport skills and tactics with consideration of athletes' current technical and tactical capabilities. This developmental progression would also apply to developing mental and life skills. For example, educator Don Hellison[9] suggests that when teaching young people personal and social responsibility, coaches and teachers work with youth to develop self-control and respectful behavior before developing other self-directed and leadership behaviors.

5. *Plan for Periods of Accelerated Adaptations to Training (Sensitive Periods).* As young people grow and mature, they become physically and mentally ready for particular types of training that accelerate adaptations during this time. Bayli and colleagues[10] describe these as sensitive periods of trainability and suggest when athletes are properly trained during these times it can "contribute significantly to the foundation of aerobic and strength development." Therefore, it is critical that coaches recognize these sensitive periods when planning for the season. While these sensitive periods are unique to each individual athlete, Rhodri Lloyd and Jon Oliver's (2012) Youth Physical Development Model[11] and Bayli and colleagues'[12] work on long-term development provide general indicators for identifying these sensitive periods. While it is helpful for coaches to recognize these periods

of accelerated adaptations to training, it is equally important for coaches to develop physical literacy, flexibility, skills, speed, endurance, power, and strength throughout youth sport training.

6. *Set Guidelines for Specialization and Competition Training.* Current best practices in youth sport suggest multisport participation should be encouraged throughout childhood, and competitive experiences should be moderated by age.[13] While this varies based on the sport, coaches are encouraged to review guidelines provided by their national governing bodies and coaches' associations. For example, the United States Olympic and Paralympic Committee[14] has recommended, through its American Development Model, athletes try multiple sports in their younger years (under 12) and even in high school continue with more than one sport. In fact, the only time they recommend single sport participation is if an athlete is training at the elite level. Canada, in their Sport for Life *Long-Term Development in Sport and Physical Activity* framework,[15] recommends kids younger than nine years old engage in play and unstructured activities rather than formal competitions.

7. *Know Your Athletes' Motives and Capabilities.* Finally, every person entering a sport setting as an athlete will have a different trajectory. For example, some individuals will develop competencies that will help them participate in sport at a high level (e.g., the Olympics) while others will use their competencies to enjoy being physically active throughout their life. Both are admirable goals, but the crux is that it is the role of youth sport coaches and youth sport administrators to help any individual joins their team or program to become physically literate, improve in the sport, and, for some, attempt excellence in their sport. Therefore, youth coaches will need to recognize that while all of their athletes want to develop and challenge themselves, few will train and compete at the high school level and even fewer will excel at a high-performance level. This is an important consideration in planning goals and expectations within the team or program.

Utilizing these key concepts of long-term athlete development can help the coach create a season or program that will meet their athletes' developmental needs. Further, by reviewing these concepts, coaches should be able to recognize and plan their programs to promote athlete development that matches the athletes' growth and maturation patterns. Below is an example of how Brianna, the swim coach, might plan for coaching practice using the principles of long-term development.

RETURNING TO THE CASE OF BRIANNA THE SWIM COACH

With an understanding of long-term development, Brianna and the Sharks Swim Club administrators can refine athlete development outcomes and plan for how they will develop athletes in the program and throughout the season. Here is how they could implement the seven points noted:

1. *Focus on Physical Literacy.* While Sharks swimmers have developed the fundamental motor skill of swimming, Brianna will continue to refine their stroke technique and help them develop knowledge of the sport. However, where she could spend more time is continuing to build the confidence and motivation of her swimmers as well as create practices and a deck atmosphere that is fun and enjoyable.

2. *Use Developmentally Appropriate Spaces, Equipment, and Competitive Structures.* Brianna is already well prepared. She accommodates different size and stature by having a variety of sizes of fins, kickboards, and paddles available for her swimmers. She also plans practices based on their current endurance and speed capabilities having them adjust times accordingly. Brianna is also aware of the early and late maturers on her team and really spends time focusing on individual improvement both during practices and at meets.

3. *Plan Season or Program Based on Athlete Developmental Pathway.* As a USA Swimming Member Coach, Brianna has received information on the American Development Model (ADM).[16] She also has the USA Swimming ADM Level 1–6 Exit Competencies,[17] which outline the biomechanical progressions, psychological progressions, character and life skills, and mental skills for each level emphasizing the holistic development of the swimmers. Prior to the start of the upcoming season, she works with her assistant coaches to identify the current level of each athlete. They discover their swimmers fall into Levels 3–5. Therefore, they will plan their season around these levels.

4. *Create a Progression of Development within the Sport Season.* The bulk of Brianna's planning time is spent considering how best to progress biomechanical and physiological development over the course of the season, as well as considering how she will incorporate life skills and mental skills into her weekly practice plans. Therefore, she sets aside a few weekend time slots to work with her assistant coaches to develop season plans based on each of the ADM levels, building progression over the course of the season.

5. *Plan for Periods of Accelerated Adaptations to Training (Sensitive Periods).* Given that Brianna coaches 11–14 year-old swimmers, she recognizes many of her athletes may begin or are in a sensitive period for accelerated adaptations in endurance, speed, and strength training. Therefore, Brianna will plan to work on endurance, speed, and strength training more with the older (i.e., high school age) athletes.

6. *Set Guidelines for Specialization and Competition Training.* Brianna would want to make sure to continue to encourage multisport participation and remind her athletes about how other sports can help them learn how to push themselves, compete, and work as a team. In regard to competition, Brianna will want to increase the amount of physical and muscular training from what they have had in previous years by introducing speed intervals, scheduled strength training, and increased opportunities to compete against their teammates in training sessions.

7. *Know Your Athletes' Motives and Capabilities.* As Brianna knows that not all her athletes will swim competitively in high school or college, she wants to focus on helping each athlete develop and improve as they go through the swim program, as well as enjoy swimming as an activity throughout their lifetime.

DEVELOPING PHYSICAL CONDITIONING

One key component of the planning process for youth sport coaches is physical conditioning. A physical conditioning program implemented by coaches can increase endurance, boost confidence, reduce injuries, and aid in recovery, all of which lead to better performance.[18] However, one size does not fit all when it comes to designing physical conditioning programs and in youth sport, both context and the maturation of the young athlete matter. For example, prepubescent youth participating in a community youth basketball program need a different type of physical conditioning plan than middle school basketball players. Furthermore, a U16 club volleyball team expects their physical conditioning component will complement their volleyball skill training. In addition to the age of the athletes, there are many components for coaches to consider when planning a physical conditioning program, including body composition, current fitness level, flexibility, strength, speed, and power.[19] Prior to planning a physical conditioning program that fits the context they work in and the athletes they work with, coaches should ask themselves the following questions:

- What legal responsibilities do I have in planning a physical conditioning program for my athletes?
- What ethical responsibilities do I have in planning a physical conditioning program for my athletes?
- What physical skills do my athletes currently possess?
- What is the maturation level of my athletes, based on their age and current physical development?
- What are the best practices for training athletes in my sport, relative to the setting I work in?

Once coaches have considered the previous questions, they are now ready to prepare their physical conditioning program around best practices and training principles. Some common mistakes youth coaches make when planning physical conditioning programs is "too much, too fast" (overtraining), lack of specificity (the training is too general), or they have limited knowledge of current or best practices (e.g., when to apply static and dynamic stretching). To overcome this, youth coaches can use six commonly used training principles: (1) overload, (2) progression, (3) specificity, (4) individualization, (5) periodization, and (6) reversibility.[20] Each of the six training principles are described below and accompanied by an example of how they can be implemented into a physical training program.

1. *Overload.* The deliberate increase of training stress or physical intensity to challenge athletes to go beyond normal physical performance.[21] The overload principle can be implemented to increase power. For example, a

tennis instructor might increase the number of tennis balls used in ball-retrieval sprints. Ball-retrieval sprints are a drill where players sprint to retrieve tennis balls placed by the net, one at a time, and return them to the baseline.

2. *Progression.* Planned increase in training load to improve performance over time.[22] For instance, when a U16 lacrosse club coach gradually increases the amount of weight her athletes are lifting during squat exercises in the weight room, she is utilizing progression in training.

3. *Specificity.* Designing the training program exercises to align with the activities used in the sport the athlete is training for. If a middle school football coach has his athletes complete a three-mile run each week, this would have limited specificity to the activities of playing football. Whereas, a volleyball coach implementing exercises to develop the athletes' power when jumping would be using specificity-training principles.

4. *Individualization.* Adjusting the training principles for each athlete, based on a variety of factors, including age, current fitness level, and confidence. In youth sport, a high school wrestling coach would assess athletes' current level of fitness at the beginning of preseason and in-season workouts to account for variations in athletes' fitness levels as some athletes might be coming from fall sports or may be new to the sport, such as incoming athletes.

5. *Periodization.* Creating variation in the training program over time.[23] This includes manipulation of the other training principles. A middle school cross country coach might decrease or pause the number of walking lunge repetitions during the strength-training session two weeks prior to the citywide meet to allow the athletes to recover and avoid muscle fatigue.

6. *Reversibility.* The result of an athlete losing previous gains from a physical conditioning program.[24] In youth sport, summer vacations, holiday breaks, and other school activities could cause an athlete to see decrease in muscle tissue or endurance capacity. Coaches can provide take-home activities to reduce reversibility, encourage multisport participation, or offer offseason workouts to accommodate those not participating in other sports.

Here is an explanation of how Brianna can implement the six training principles, in her in-season, 10-week physical conditioning program:

1. *Overload.* Brianna demonstrates the overload principle by testing her athletes at the beginning of the season and then creating workouts that will slightly overload where they are currently in their swimming fitness.

2. *Progression.* To engage in progression throughout the 10-week program, Brianna can plan to increase the distance across the 10 weeks by increasing the number of sets. For example, starting with 5 × 100 meters and concluding with 15 × 100 meters. Alternatively, she could keep the rest and the distance the same, but ask swimmers to hold a repeat time that is faster. For example, repeat a set of 10 × 100's the first time hold 1:12 and then next time hold 1:09.

3. *Specificity.* To assist with muscular strength Brianna could have her swimmers engage in an exercise that align with activities related to swimming to improve the athletes' performance such as shoulder internal/external rotation.

4. *Individualization.* While the 10-week program is designed for all athletes across the U14 club team, Brianna could adjust one or more of the activities to better match an athlete's current fitness level. For example, a swimmer with less conditioning would do fewer repetitions of a set or have a slower interval compared to other athletes with higher levels of conditioning. Additionally, if one of her athletes is coming back from a shoulder injury, she may want to limit the intensity or adjust the frequency of the muscular-strength exercises. In another example, not all athletes may be able to do standard push-ups. Thus, the athletes could be allowed to do push-ups using a different approach, such as on their knees.

5. *Periodization.* Since the 10-week physical conditioning program is going to be implemented in-season, Brianna may want to consider manipulating a few of the training principles to improve competitive performance. For example, she might skip the third day of physical or muscular-endurance training during a week leading up to a competition to give her athletes a little more time to recover.

6. *Reversibility.* There may be a weekend with no competition or a period of three to four days with no practice time, perhaps due to a holiday. In this case, Brianna could provide take-home exercises related to muscular endurance and encourage her U14 athletes to complete them to continue maintaining muscular strength.

PLANNING TRAINING AROUND COMPETITIVE STRATEGIES

Another area youth sport coaches plan for is how to implement competitive strategies. Competitive strategies are the tactics used in competition to improve the team's chances of winning against their opponent. Each sport has a variety of strategies coaches can implement. For example, a soccer coach teaches a possession strategy, an offensive strategy to control the ball and deny the opposition possession of the ball; a youth basketball coach employs a pressing person-to-person defense to change the pace of the game and utilize the team's speed and quickness; and a youth baseball coach teaches players the "hit and run" to implement an aggressive offensive mind-set.

The act of planning competitive strategies involves combining the individual technical skills of athletes with specific tactics to defeat an opponent. Before planning which strategies to use and how to teach them, coaches will first need to become competent in knowing the type of strategies commonly used in their sport. There are many resources, through sport organizations, available to coaches in regard to the types of competitive strategy they can implement in their sport (see chapter 11).

Second, youth sport coaches need to be able to relate competitive strategies appropriately to the setting in which they are coaching. For example, a high school basketball coach could teach a switching zone defense to improve her team's chance at making the state tournament, whereas a community youth coach would want to teach person-to-person defense to focus on basic individual defensive skills (e.g., balance, defensive stance, positioning, sliding your feet).

Sport researchers Amy Price, Dave Collins, John Stoszkowski, and Shane Pill[25] discuss a variety of factors that influence preparing athletes for competitive situations. They include the following:

- the current ability of the athletes to make real-time decisions and anticipate the actions of their teammates and the opposition,
- the specific tactical aspects unique to each sport,
- the norms of the game or how the game is played within the rules of the game,
- self-awareness of the players in regard to their own abilities, and
- individual athlete awareness of their teammates' abilities.

In sum, when planning for teaching game strategy, the youth coach needs to consider their athletes' background in the sport relative to their age level and whether the sport is participation or performance based. Once coaches are clear about the athletes' background, age level, and the setting, they can teach game strategy using the following progression:

1. Teach the rules of the game. Plan time during each practice to provide instruction on the official rules of playing the sport using the official rulebook associated with their sport and context.
2. Implement game scenarios. To help athletes in their ability to reflect and adapt to ever-changing game situations, coaches can plan competitive practice activities that mimic game scenarios. For example, a basketball coach might plan a game where athletes are faced with a trapping, pressing defense to get the ball across half-court. In this particular game, the athletes advance their individual skills, such as dribbling and passing, while preparing for teams that use a pressing style of play.
3. Teach basic tactical skills. To prepare athletes to meet the norms of the game or how the game is played within the rules, coaches will want to incorporate instructional time to explain the nuances of playing the sport. For example, a basketball coach could inform their athletes how defensive players set a screen to slow the offensive player.
4. Instill the coach's style of play. Based on their coaching philosophy, coaches will set aside specific time in practice to teach their style of play. As previously mentioned, a youth soccer coach might teach a possession strategy to control the ball and deny the opposition possession of the ball.
5. Prepare for an upcoming opponent. As a sport moves from a participation-based model to a more competitive level, coaches will plan a portion of practice, often a practice session or two before an upcoming contest, to share information with their team on what to expect from an upcoming opponent. This may include a scouting report and/or the use of a scout team to run the opponent's offensive or defensive strategy.

While coaches can use the above progressive sequence in planning to teach game strategy, the actual teaching of competitive strategy will also be influenced by the instructional approach used by the coach (see chapter 8).

PLANNING FOR MENTAL SKILLS TRAINING

In addition to planning for athletes' physical development for the sport, coaches will also want to plan for athletes' development of mental skills. Mental skills are those activities or tools coaches can use to train athletes' thoughts and behaviors to allow the athletes to regulate their mental state.[26] Example mental states include being confident and determined, having an optimal energy and arousal level for competition, performing under pressure, engaging in the right type of focus, adapting to change, and being a team player. The role of the coach is to consider how best to plan and teach these mental skills through the season. The following steps can be useful in this endeavor.

1. *Choose the mental states.* While coaches may be tempted to focus on all of the mental states, it is important to consider the age of the athlete. For example, performing under pressure may be less of a concern for younger athletes who have fewer competitions. In addition, a coach may have experience with the athletes in previous seasons and may be able to recognize when athletes on the team get overanxious they perform poorly and could use help managing arousal. Further, Vealey[27] suggests practitioners may want to start with foundational states like determination and confidence, then progress to performance states like anxiety and focus, and lastly progress to personal and team states such as communication and team chemistry.

2. *Choose the mental skills.* There are a variety of ways to improve mental states. Some of the most recommended skills in the sport psychology literature are arousal regulation techniques, goal setting, imagery, self-talk, and concentration techniques. It will be important for coaches to learn about these skills and how they may be applied in practice. Additionally, coaches want to make sure to consider the age and experience of the athlete when determining how the skill might be introduced. For example, deep breathing, an arousal regulation technique, may help athletes of any age relax and regain focus after making a mistake. However, a 9-year-old may better learn deep breathing by talking about making your belly rise like a balloon and placing your hand on your belly to see it rise. In turn, a 14-year-old may be fine being reminded to keep the shoulders down and push their belly out when they breathe in.

3. *Incorporate mental skills into practice.* When teaching mental skills, coaches want to follow the same protocol as teaching physical skills. That

is, start with the basics and then progressively build the skill over time. Additionally, coaches want to consider the cognitive and social development of the athlete. For example, younger athletes will benefit from concrete and simple explanations. Here is a sample protocol for coaches to consider implementing in practice.

1. Educate athletes about the skill by telling them what it is and why it is important to learn.
2. Teach the mental skill keeping it simple, concrete, and fun.
3. Have the athletes use the skill repeatedly across practice sessions.
4. Introduce additional complexity to the skill and again use the skill in practice.
5. Once the skill has been developed and practiced across several weeks, implement it into a game situation.

See table 7.2 for examples of how coaches, like Brianna, can progressively introduce mental skills into their sport season. Additionally, coaches can see in the example that multiple mental states may be addressed by the same mental skill.

Table 7.2. Sample Mental Skill Training Progression

Mental State	First Three Weeks	Middle Three Weeks	Last Four Weeks
Confidence performing under pressure	Discuss the importance of confidence and the role of self-talk and support in building confidence. Encourage athletes to focus on what they can do and provide encouragement to teammates.	Have a parent observe a practice and competition to monitor supportive comments. Have athletes share their self-talk statements to post during competitions. Have a parent video record competitions and create a highlight reel that highlights great actions for all athletes.	Encourage athletes to take risks and use their self-talk and team support in pressure situations and highlight successes to maintain and build confidence.
Attentional focus performing under pressure	Discuss importance of letting mistakes go during competitions and develop a mistake ritual and use during practices.	Apply mistake ritual during competitions and evaluate how it is working. Make changes, if needed.	Keep using the mistake ritual.

Mental State	First Three Weeks	Middle Three Weeks	Last Four Weeks
Determination confidence	Remind athletes of goals they have set in previous seasons and discuss use of short- and long-term goals. Meeting in small groups (maybe by distance or stroke), develop short- and long-term goals for three skills they want to improve.	Check in on short-term goals and make adjustments. Ask athletes to identify strategies they can use to help them meet their goals.	Check in on short-term goals and make final adjustments and see how their strategies are working. During final week, check in on long-term goals and share all improvements with the team.

PLANNING FOR LIFE-SKILL DEVELOPMENT

Building life skills is also considered a valuable reason for young athletes to participate in sports. To help facilitate this process, coaches can also plan for life-skill development. Life skills are defined as competencies that young people can develop to help them be more successful in their communities (school, sport, home, local community, etc.).[28] The following are examples of life skills: teamwork, leadership, goal setting, problem solving, communication, time management, and emotional regulation.[29] As coaches review this list, they will probably recognize these are valuable skills for youth in the sport setting and may even recognize that participating in sport can help young people develop these skills. However, researchers have found that just participating in sport does not guarantee life-skill development, rather it requires coaches actively work to develop these life skills alongside technical and tactical skills.[30]

The process of developing life skills is akin to developing physical and mental skills. Here are the steps outlined by practitioners in coach education:[31,32]

1. *Choose the life skills.* Coaches need to consider what life skills they want to develop during the season. Just like with developing technical sport skills, coaches need to consider what is developmentally appropriate for their athletes and how many new skills they can reasonably develop in a given season.
2. *Define each life skill.* Coaches will need to develop brief definitions to help the athletes understand the life skill and how it will be applied in the sport setting. Then coaches want to help athletes remember the life skills by creating signs/posters that highlight each of the team's life skills. For example,

if responsibility is a life skill, a 11–12 age group swimming coach might define it as a question posted on the pool deck that reads, "Responsibility—What action are *you* taking today to be a better swimmer?"

3. *Make team rules that align with life skills.* Coaches may also set team rules that align with their life skills. For responsibility, a 11–12 age group swimming coach might create rules related to showing up ready to get in the water by practice start time with all of their equipment (e.g., fins, paddles, snorkel, water bottle, googles, extra caps) in tow. If coaches do set rules, they will want to set consequences when the rules are violated.

4. *Build a positive coach-athlete relationship.* When coaches build a positive relationship with athletes they get to know their needs, interests, and capabilities. In doing so, coaches can be more effective in helping their athletes develop life skills. For example, a 11–12 age group swimming coach may know one of the swimmers, Oscar, struggles with confidence, continually questioning his swimming ability and setting low training goals for himself. By knowing this about Oscar, the coach knows to spend time building his confidence. The coach can do this by showing Oscar his training times, verbalizing a belief that he can improve the times, and encouraging him to take action during practice to push himself a little harder. When Oscar does push himself in practice, the coach is there to praise his attempts. Without knowing Oscar and taking the time to support Oscar's confidence, it would be unlikely Oscar would take responsibility to improve his own training in practice. Therefore, building a positive coach-athlete relationship allows the coach to mentor athletes and help them develop life skills.

5. *Create a climate that fosters effort and improvement.* When coaches create a climate that fosters effort and improvement it reminds athletes that they can develop. It also helps the athlete be more responsible, be a better leader, and be more in control of their emotions. What is required for coaches is to help athletes learn what it means to apply effort, encourage application of effort in practice and competition, and strategize ways to improve.

6. *Develop practices with a life skill in mind.* Just as coaches plan practices to focus on particular technical and tactical skills, they should also do the same for life skills. Here are some things to keep in mind:

- Choose the life skill for the day.
- During the brief introduction to what practice will be like for the day, discuss the life skill (1–2 minutes).

- During practice praise athletes using the life skill.
- Pick one drill, set, or small-sided game that will emphasize the life skill. As athletes practice, provide feedback on the life skill.
- During the brief conclusion to practice, in two to three minutes, discuss the life skill. For example, reinforce how it was used well in practice, what could be better, and how it will help them in sport or other areas of life. Coaches can also question athletes on what they learned, highlight examples of the life skill in action, ask them to rate themselves on how well they used the life skill, and ask them to talk about other settings where they might use the skill.

REVISIT THE SCENARIO WITH BRIANNA

Here is how Brianna might introduce life-skill development on her team using the following approach at the start of practice:

Brianna: Today we are going to focus on responsibility. What is responsibility?

(Athletes respond)

Brianna: Yes, that is right. It is each of you taking action to become a better swimmer. Today in practice we are going to focus on our responsibility, and in particular, challenge ourselves to be better. Do you remember that set of 10 × 100's we did three weeks ago? Today we are going to do that same set on a quicker interval. So if you did them on 1:40 last time you will do them on 1:37 this time. Are you ready for the challenge?

(Athletes nod in agreement)

Brianna: I think you are. Let's get started with warm-up.

During the 10 × 100 set, Brianna would walk around encouraging swimmers to take action to challenge themselves and push themselves to be better. At the end of practice she would have another brief discussion:

Brianna: Wow, I am proud of you today. You all took responsibility to make yourself better today. You each pushed yourselves to go faster and even if you did not finish all 10 on time, you kept with it and did not give up. Well done! Being responsible for your own training is an important skill in swimming, but can you think about how this might apply to school or at home?

(Athletes respond)

Brianna: Great example. We can improve how we do in school by being responsible and completing our homework as soon as we get home each day. Again, great workout, team cheer on three.

Overall, it is clear that to develop life skills coaches are modeling, teaching, and reinforcing these skills. The important thing for coaches to keep in mind is to be intentional in developing these skills.

CONCLUSION

In sum, coaches can improve their longevity as a coach and create a positive environment for youth to develop through intentional planning that includes progression in athlete development, designing conditioning programs, outlining competitive strategies for the season, and creating mental and life-skill training programs. In addition, regardless of the youth sport setting coaches work in, table 7.3 offers a checklist that can be used to help coaches plan daily practice or training sessions, create season plans, and design offseason workouts.

Table 7.3. Planning Checklist

The following skills are included . . .	
	Tactical skills
	Technical skill
	Physical conditioning
	Mental skills
	Life skills
Each activity is deliberately designed to . . .	
	Achieve a desired outcome relative to skill development
	Be developmentally appropriate for the current skill level and age of the athlete
	Improve the individual skills of each athlete using the appropriate developmental sequence
Additional considerations:	
	Opportunities for athlete-to-athlete social interaction are included when possible
	Each session and/or activity is focused on athlete development
	An understanding of why the athletes are participating has been determined

PLAN TO COACH

Much of how I prep for practice sessions stems from my background as a classroom teacher. My daily habit of lesson planning, aligned with my long-term vision of where I wanted my students to arrive at the end of the academic year, is no different than how I plan out each practice with my basketball team so that they are playing at their peak at the end of the season. At the micro level, this means that there are certain routines we use all the time, regardless of what point in the season, such as dynamic warm-ups, footwork drills, and shooting drills, both stationary and on the move. Moving to the macro level, the objective is for our players to become problem solvers who can "figure it out" when the script is thrown out the window during the pressures of playoff basketball. The planning part for the coach comes in setting up exercises rather than drills, where players must collaborate and communicate in situational scenarios to manage time and score. Similar to how teaching trends in the classroom has moved toward group work and student decision making, basketball coaches must adapt and find ways to empower their players to make their own decisions on the court.

—Marshall Cho, head boys' basketball coach,
Lake Oswego High School (OR)

HELPING COACHES PLAN

We believe that our coaches are knowledgeable and lifelong learners, so we try to focus on things that happen beyond the practices and games to help them be more efficient. We have developed an internal athletic-resource webpage to help the coach manage all of the things that go into coaching. The coaches can login to

(continued)

HELPING COACHES PLAN (*continued*)

the athletic resource page at any time and find preseason checklist, banquet checklist, professional development opportunities, postseason and team travel, the Leander ISD coaches handbook, and their UIL district rules. This site is made with our coaches in mind, so if there is something that they think would be helpful, we will add it. The goal is that if we can provide easily accessed information, the coach will be able to use their time to plan for their team and athletes' success. In addition, we think that planning and learning how to manage a season starts before they become a head coach. Thus, during our in district professional development time we have created a session, "Beyond the X's and O's." This session is geared to what is required in being a head coach and is directed at assistant coaches that have the aspirations of becoming a head coach. We also encourage our head coaches to invest time in their assistant coaches by giving them responsibilities and opportunities to grow. Prior to the season we will bring in all the head coaches from one sport across all six of our high schools. This is structured time for coaches to spend time with each other and the athletic office to discuss sport-specific information in preparation for the upcoming season.

—Jon Lamb, athletic director, Leander ISD (Texas)

COACH TIPS!

- Schedule and make time to plan for the upcoming season and for daily practice sessions.
- Plan for the teaching of technical skill progression by utilizing long-term development concepts.
- Plan for the teaching of physical conditioning by implementing the six commonly used training principles. They are overload, progression, specificity, individualization, periodization, and reversibility.

- Plan for the teaching of competitive strategies by using a progression that includes the teaching of game rules, implementing practice scenarios, teaching of basic tactical skills, teaching the norms of the game, and preparing for an upcoming opponent.
- Plan for the teaching of mental skill training by selecting a few key mental skills to implement during the season, repeatedly in practices and then in competition.
- Plan for the teaching of life-skill development by making time to recognize and discuss life skills during practice sessions.

COACH DEVELOPER TIPS!

- Schedule a time with coaches to discuss planning for the upcoming season.
- Encourage coaches to share season plans and set up a time to discuss how they align with planning principles from the chapter.
- Provide coaches resources on how to teach technical skill progression, physical conditioning, and competitive strategies relative to their sport.
- Provide coaches resources on how to implement mental skill training and life-skill development relative to the age of the athletes and ask them to identify the skills they plan to implement during the season.

8

To Coach Is to Teach

The role of youth sport coaches involves a variety of skills and abilities, including, but not limited to, leadership, organization, planning, and communication. The responsibility to apply each skill and ability will vary based on the coaching context. For example, a volunteer parent coach of a U8 softball team will not employ the skill of planning to the same extent as a high school softball coach. However, the one skill all coaches need to develop, regardless of the context they work in, is the ability to teach. While the connection to teaching and coaching are logical, unless coaches are trained educators, they may have limited knowledge of best practices in learning principles.

COACH FLEMING'S DILEMMA

Danyelle Fleming was excited about her new coaching position at Northside Middle School. She was the new head eighth-grade girls' basketball coach, one year after serving as an assistant coach, but she was a bit nervous that she was not quite ready for the job as she walked out of the preseason coaches meeting. Danyelle had already planned out the drills she would use to teach the fundamental skills of basketball. She had also outlined the defensive and offensive systems she would implement, but during the meeting the athletic director had both the varsity boys' and the varsity girls' basketball coach at the high school speak on how they taught basketball skills and strategy to their varsity athletes. The girls' coach shared how she used guided discovery as her teaching approach, with a focus on game-based learning. Danyelle had never heard of either guided discovery or game-based learning. She just assumed every coach introduced a new skill by explaining what the skill was and how to use it and then provide a demonstration of the skill; the players would practice the skill and the coach would provide feedback. This is how every coach she had been around taught the game. Now with only a few days away from the first practice, she started asking herself some questions. Should I be using guided discovery? What other methods are there I don't know about? How do I learn more about this?

IMPLEMENTING AN INSTRUCTIONAL STYLE

The effectiveness of the teaching approach implemented by coaches is predicated on their ability to connect with the learner (see chapter 4), nurture an inclusive and positive environment (chapter 5), create a safe practice setting (chapter 6), and plan to provide structured and developmentally appropriate practice sessions to teach skills and competitive strategy (chapter 7). In addition, the approach taken by coaches will be guided by their coach philosophy (chapter 1) and the standards of performance they establish for their team (chapter 2). While coaches have a variety of instructional styles to use (see table 8.1), coaches will want to consider whether an athlete-centered compared to coach-centered style produces the desired learning and motivational outcomes. A coach-centered style is a reproduction of knowledge where the coach teaches a skill and the athlete reproduces the skill in the form of practice.[1] When coaches focus on providing athletes with more autonomy in problem solving and overcoming challenges on the field of play, they are using an athlete-centered instructional style that produces new knowledge.[2]

One athlete-centered instructional style that works well in youth sport is the game-based approach.[3] In the game-based instructional approach, coaches place athletes in a position to make decisions while they become a facilitator of the learning process.[4] Authors Alan Launder and Wendy Piltz[5] frame the game-based instructional approach around the concepts of focusing, shaping, enhancing, and freezing play. *Focusing play* is when coaches determine the objective or what specific technique, tactic, or aspect of an athlete's conditioning they are going to teach relative to a tactical problem in competitive play. *Shaping play* is when the coach organizes the game or activity to align with what they are going to teach. Shaping play might include using modifications

Table 8.1. Common Instructional Styles

Style	Coach/Athlete Centered	Description*
Command	Coach-centered	The coach is the decision maker and athletes are motivated and expected to follow the decisions made by the coach.[1]
Inclusion	Coach-centered	The coach plans all activities, but designs varying degrees of difficulty and then allows the athlete to have a more individualized learning experience based on their current skill level and social and emotional development.[2]
Practice	Coach-centered	The coach provides specific instruction, then through observation provides individual and private feedback to the athlete.[3]
Reciprocal	Coach-centered	The coach provides a social setting in which athletes can observe other athletes learning and they can offer peer feedback as an observer. The coach provides feedback only through the observer.[4]
Guided discovery**	Athlete-centered	The coach designs games and poses a sequence of challenges and questions to lead athletes to discover the correct response themselves.[5]
Learner-initiated***	Athlete-centered	The coach accepts the athlete's role as an independent learner, providing support as the athlete drives the learning experience.[6]

Notes:
*The word *coach* is used in place of the word *teacher* and the word *athlete* in place of the word *student*, in the description of each teaching style to align with the youth sport setting.
**Guided discovery is referred to as the game-based approach in coaching.
***Learner-initiated instructional styles expand on the guided discovery approach by placing more responsibility with the student-athlete to guide the learning process.

Sources:
1. Melissa Jensen, "Pedagogy of Coaching," in *Coaching for Sports Performance*, ed. Timothy Baghurst (New York: Routledge, 2020), 50.
2. Muska Mosston and Sara Ashworth, *Teaching Physical Education: First Online Edition* (United States: Spectrum Institute for Teaching and Learning, 2008), 156.
3. Mosston and Ashworth, 98.
4. Mosston and Ashworth, 116.
5. Mosston and Ashworth., 213.
6. Mosston and Ashworth, 283.

to equipment, implementing small-sided games, adjusting the rules of play, and/or altering the scoring system. With *enhancing play*, coaches try to keep all athletes on task and active during the game as well as enhance the activity by providing progressive challenges to improve skills within competition. In *freezing play*, coaches pause activity and, based on their observation, reflect with their athletes using guiding questions to help them discover ways to improve their physical and mental skills as well as decision making.

Danyelle, in the previous scenario, could implement a game-based approach in teaching the fundamentals of basketball to her eighth-grade team. This method would nurture each athlete's decision-making skills and help them transfer the skill to competitive play. For example, Danyelle wants her athletes to get better at moving without the ball, a skill that requires footwork, the ability to change speed of pace, and reading the movement of other players on the court. While Danyelle could plan simple drills that focus on the specifics of each skill, she decides to use the game-based approach to design a game that combines all three components of moving without the ball while challenging her athletes to make game-like decisions and practice basic skills. Table 8.2 provides an example of a game-based approach for learning to move without the ball by incorporating live offensive and defensive play designed to improve athlete skills.

Table 8.2. Game-Based Instructional Example

Focus play: Describe tactical situations related to objective and tactical options	
Game	Three-on-three moving without dribbling the basketball.
Tactical objective	For athletes to read the defense (understanding angles) and respond with appropriate footwork (balance, plant, and cut) and change of pace to create space from defender and be open to receive a pass.
Shape play: Develop practice organization	
Set-up	• Half-court, one basket, one ball. • (Three) athletes on offense, (three) on defense, rotating athletes on the baseline.
Rules of play	• No dribbling. • Must cut after a pass. • Athletes must square to the basketball upon catching the ball. • Make it–take it. The team on offense keeps the ball if they score, the offense rotates off the court if they lose possession, new defense rotates in from the baseline. • The ball is checked through the coach after a score or change of possession.
Enhance play: Keep athletes active and challenge them to relate basic skills to the competitive setting	
The flow of the game	• Eight-minute continuous game. • After a score or change in possession, athletes rotate in from the baseline on defense after a quick rest of 10 to 25 seconds. • Between each game the coach adds a new challenge. For example: 1. Each player on offense must touch the ball twice before an attempt to score.

	2. Offensive team only has 10 seconds to attempt to score.
	3. Offensive players can now dribble, but can only attempt a score off of a pass (i.e., pass-cut-receive-shoot, catch and shoot).
Freeze play: Observe, pause, and reflect with athletes, then adjust and repeat the activity	
Pause and reinforce key teaching points	• When needed, she freezes play and provides guiding questions related to reading the defender, footwork, and change of pace, sample questions include:
	1. When the ball moved from the top of the middle of the court to the sideline, how did your defender adjust to see the ball and you? At what angle might you move to create space from the defender to receive a pass?
	2. After making the pass, which foot did you lead with to make your cut?
	3. When making your cut to get open, when would have been a better time to change your pace to create more space between you and your defender?
	• Play is resumed.
	• Provide group and individual feedback focused on the tactical objective. For example,
	1. Creating space away from the defender to receive a pass.
	2. Using the correct footwork when making a cut to create space.
	3. Squaring to the basket when receiving a pass.
	4. Reading the defender when creating space or making a cut.
Focus play: Revisit the practice objective at completion of the game	
Debrief questions for athletes	1. Why is it important to square to the basket when we catch the ball?
	2. Why do we want to cut after making a pass?
	3. What might be some reasons why you were not open to receive a pass?
	4. What do we need to remember when making a cut to get open?

Regardless of the instructional style used, coaches will want to make sure the approach implemented leads to the advancement of athlete skills through a progression of structured drills and activities. However, for youth sport coaches to become more effective teachers when they design instructional sessions, it is also important for them to consider how to provide demonstrations, create activities focused on repetition and game-based decision-making skills, and provide effective feedback.

DEVELOPING AUTONOMY THROUGH COACHING METHODOLOGY

The last thing coaches need to provide youth are too many words that create the dreaded "paralysis by analysis." Better coaching methodology involves creativity and basic household items to foster a rich problem-solving environment for youth athletes. For example, using a PVC pipe, I can create a situation for teaching proper ground ball positioning for baseball or softball infielders. I start by creating an A-shaped frame with the PVC pipe. Then I have the athlete assume their fielding position; their shins can't touch the lower horizontal bar and their upper back cannot touch the upper horizontal bar, creating a perfect hip hinge position with the body and forcing their hands out in front of them when fielding. A PVC pipe can be used for teaching hitting mechanics, as well. A common drill I use to teach proper arm path and positioning is putting a 12" PVC pipe between their elbows during the swing. Their goal is simply to hit the ball hard over the pitcher's head. The PVC pipe between the elbows forces proper arm angles (front elbow goes up and back elbow goes down during the swing to create an upward arc of the bat), rotation coming from the torso, and late-to-absent wrist roll-over, with which all three create proper bat path and power output. Over the years, I've definitely found that kids enjoy the use of props, like the PVC pipe, more so than me simply telling them what to do and what to feel during the drill. This type of coaching also provides a bit of autonomy to the youth athlete as they try and figure movements out on their own. It fosters movement exploration and increased body awareness.

—Dr. Cisco Reyes, U12 head softball coach, Oregon Blaze

THE IMPORTANCE OF DEMONSTRATIONS

While the teaching of sport skills will depend on the method coaches adopt, all teaching styles in sport require the coach to provide some type of demonstration of a skill or tactic. By watching another person model a skill, athletes gather information that can help them learn how to do the skill or tactic. Albert Bandura postulated social learning theory[6] to explain how individuals learn through observing others. In doing so, he outlined four important processes individuals should follow to facilitate learning from an observation or demonstration. These processes are attention, retention, reproduction, and reinforcement and motivation.[7] More specifically, for an athlete to learn from a coaching demonstration, the coach will need to direct the athlete toward what to attend to while not overloading attentional capacity, encourage the athlete to learn, provide opportunities for the athlete to remember the information, and give the athlete a chance to practice it while referencing the skill is being done correctly. One way to accomplish this is to use the five-step approach for demonstrating a skill, provided below. Noted within each step is how attention (A), retention (R), reproduction (P), and reinforcement and motivation (M) are incorporated to promote learning.

FIVE-STEP APPROACH FOR DEMONSTRATIONS

Step 1: Say what they will do and why

- Bring athletes together so everyone can see the person providing demonstration while limiting distractions. (A)
- Grab their attention and tell athletes what they will do (no more than one minute) (A)
- Tell athletes why learning the skill is important and/or who has used the skill (no more than one minute) (M)

Step 2: Say each of the steps

- Describe each step (2–3 minutes for all steps)

  - Do not overload. Limit to 3–4 steps with instructional cues. If needed, break into manageable sections and do remaining steps separate for each section (A, R)
  - Try to chunk information (e.g., make a story, use a mnemonic device) (A, R)

- Have athletes repeat the verbal cues including story or mnemonic device (R)

Step 3: Do each of the steps

- Physically demonstrate each step of the skill while not talking (R)
- Repeat physical demonstration and add in verbal cue (R)

Step 4: Check for understanding

- Ask athletes to summarize key points or repeat verbal cues out loud as skill is performed (R)

Step 5: Practice the skill

- Set up a quick activity to have all athletes physically practice the skill (P)
- Consider having athletes mentally practice the skill (P)
- Reinforce their successful demonstration of the skill (A, M)
- Give feedback on needed improvements and encourage athletes to continue practice (A, M)
- Create a game, drill, or activity where athletes apply the newly used skill and continue reinforcement and feedback (P, M)

In preparing to give a demonstration as outlined above, coaches will first want to consider the past experience athletes may have with the skill. For example, if this is the first time athletes are learning the skill, the coach will want to teach the simplest version of the skill and limit the number of steps and instructional cues. Additionally, coaches may want to break the skill down into manageable sections based on the concept of whole versus part learning.[8] While whole learning tends to be more beneficial, when a skill is complex it can be beneficial to break it up and teach it in parts. For example, for a complex and highly organized skill like a triple jump in track and field, a coach would progressively teach each part of the skill. However, a complex, but less organized skill, like a swim stroke, may lead a coach to teach separate parts and then put them back together again. For instance, a swim coach would teach the leg and arm movements separately in swimming before having the individual practice the whole stroke. If a skill is broken down, steps 3 through 5 in the demonstration are repeated for each section separately. Second, coaches want to review how athletes are currently doing the skill. If athletes already know how to do the skill but are struggling to perform key aspects of the skill correctly, then the demonstration would be targeted on those areas with an emphasis on correcting current practice. For example, if a basketball player is consistently not finishing his or her shots with the correct follow through, then the coach would provide a quick demonstration. Third, coaches will want to review what other similar skills the athletes already know that may help or hinder their learning. For instance, when basketball coaches teach the jump shot, they can refer back to key components of how to shoot a basketball and then focus the demonstration on how the jump shot differs from a set shot. Alternatively, if a coach teaches athletes a one-handed shot, the coach will need to consider how already knowing the two-handed shot can interfere with learning.

Another element coaches will want to consider in preparing the demonstration is how to structure the practice. In creating the quick practice activity associated with the demonstration, coaches will want to keep everyone active. There should be no standing in lines to wait to do the skill. Youth sport coaches will also want to consider whether they want to use a reciprocal style or a practice style of teaching. A reciprocal style encourages peer feedback. For example, athletes are split up into pairs and while one person does the skill, the other athlete observes and calls out the verbal cues they see their partner do. In the practice style, each athlete does the skill; if there is not enough equipment some athletes can work on form without the equipment, while the coach circulates and provides feedback. Additionally, it will be important to provide athletes enough time to practice this skill without getting bored. Therefore, coaches will want to consider how much time it may take for athletes to get the general skill memorized so they can apply it in the next practice activity (game, activity, or drill). However, keeping the drill short, no more than 5–10 minutes, depending on the complexity of the skill will be important for attentional focus. To prevent boredom, particularly for these athletes who pick up a skill quickly, coaches will want to prepare a series of challenges the athletes can move through at their own pace as they practice the skill. This is referred to as the *inclusion style*, where the coach would consider the needs of each athlete and how they will learn the skill. Once the coach feels comfortable that the athletes understand the skill, the coach will want to structure a drill, activity, or game where the athletes can apply the skill. The type of practice activity chosen here will largely be determined by the teaching style chosen by the coach.

COACH FLEMING'S DEMONSTRATION

Using a game-based approach, which includes guided discovery instructional methods, Danyelle decides to spend part of her practice working on passing. First, using a game-based approach she breaks her athletes up into four teams of three players. Two teams play on one quarter of the court and the other two teams on another quarter of the court. The goal of each team is to complete 10 passes in a row without stepping out of bounds. This game can emphasize good ball-handling skills, screening, and passing. However, Danyelle is going to focus on passing and tells her players to really work on completing good passes. As the teams begin playing, Danyelle is pinpointing players making good passes. In watching her players, she notices that no player is making a bounce pass. Danyelle realizes she needs to ask questions to help the athletes discover additional tactical options to use during the game. Therefore, she stops play and says, "Hey, I notice a lot of good chest passes here but no team has reached 10 in a row which means we have some good defense going on! But, what other ways can we pass the ball?"

(athletes respond)

Danyelle continues, "Overhead pass, bounce pass, wrap around pass, great. So why are we only using a chest pass?"

(athletes respond)

"You do most often use the overhead pass as an outlet but in addition to the chest pass we could certainly increase the number of bounce passes. Let's give it a try! When you use a bounce pass, it counts as two passes in a row" says Danyelle.

As the athletes continue the drill, almost immediately Danyelle notices that her players do not have good bounce-pass mechanics. Thus, she realizes it might be a good time for a demonstration. She stops play and brings the players into the center of the court with her back to the basket. Using the previously mentioned five-step demonstration process, Danyelle moves into a practice instructional style and begins her demonstration.

"Okay, everyone. Eyes on me," says Danyelle. "I want to give you some tips for making a great bounce pass so that when your defender is close you can pivot away and make a great bounce pass to your teammate during this game and when you compete this weekend" [*Five-Step Approach for Demonstrations, Step 1*].

"So there are four steps to a great bounce pass," says Danyelle. "First, spread the fingers; then create 'chicken wings' at your chest; next, you step-n-push; then, follow through. Let me briefly go over each one. First, spread your fingers on either side of the ball; two, create chicken wings with your elbows and place the ball at your chest; next, step forward with one foot and push the ball to the ground about three-quarters of the way to teammate; and finally, follow through by extending your arms with thumbs down." To check for understanding, Danyelle asks athletes to repeat the steps [*Five-Step Approach for Demonstrations, Step 2*].

Danyelle looks at Taylor and asks, "What is the first step?"

"Spread your fingers," says Taylor.

"Good," says Danyelle. "What is the second step, Sam?"

"Create chicken wings at your chest," says Sam.

"Great," says Danyelle. "Alright Kris, tell me what the third step is."

"Step with one foot forward and push the ball to the ground," responds Kris.

"And make sure the ball lands three-quarters of the way to the receiving player," adds Danyelle. "Now, Skyler what is the fourth step?"

"Follow-through with your thumbs down," says Skyler.

"Great work," says Danyelle. "Now that you know the steps, I will demonstrate them." Danyelle proceeds to demonstrate the skill, using each of the steps, without talking. Danyelle then says, "Now let me add the cues as I do it, (1) spread the fingers, (2) create chicken wings at chest, (3) step-n-push, and (4) follow through" [*Five-Step Approach for Demonstrations, Step 3*].

To check for understanding Danyelle says, "Okay, now I will demonstrate them again and this time I want you to say the steps as I do them."

The athletes follow along [*Five-Step Approach for Demonstrations, Step 4*].

Danyelle recognizes they are ready to practice the skill. She has the athletes pair up and complete 10 bounce passes standing about 8 feet apart. While athletes are practicing, Danyelle goes around and reinforces correct passes and provides instruction on corrections, reinforcing how they will be applied in competition [*Five-Step Approach for Demonstrations, Step 5*]. After the demonstration she has the athletes return to the 10-pass game and applauds as they begin to use the bounce pass and rack up more points.

TEACHING TACTICAL SKILLS FOR COMPETITIVE SUCCESS

In addition to teaching technical skills, coaches teach tactical skills or strategic skills in preparation for competition with another opponent. Tactical skills include, but are not limited to, knowing the rules of play, knowing your opponent's strengths and weaknesses, having the ability to read an upcoming play or game situation, and making correct decisions to gain a competitive advantage.[9] Thus, in designing practice activities, coaches consider how they are going to improve athletes' tactical awareness to help them make better tactical decisions during competitive play.[10] Tactical awareness is the ability to recognize situations during a contest and make adjustments or employ a strategy to achieve competitive success.[11] For example, in basketball, a competitive strategy is when the defense applies a full-court press. Tactical awareness by the offensive team is being able to recognize the type of press the offensive team is running. Tactical decision making is the ability of athletes to make in-game decisions on their own.[12] For example, using the same scenario where a defensive team is applying a full-court press, a player trained in tactical decision making would be able to read the type of full-court pressure being applied by the defense and lead the team to adapt their offensive press breaker to counter the competitive strategy employed by the defensive team.

Coaches can teach tactical skills and decision making by using the game-based approach described earlier. For example, Danyelle, the eighth-grade girls' basketball coach, can create a game-like scenario where the purpose is to work on set plays, using the following approach:

1. Organize athletes into four groups, with five to seven athletes per group.
2. Place one team on offense, one team on defense at one end of the court, and another team on defense at the other end of the court. The fourth group occupies a spot on a baseline.
3. The offensive team takes the ball at half-court, facing one direction. The offensive team has 20 seconds to score. If they score they keep the ball and move in the opposite direction against a new defense waiting at the other end of the court. If they lose possession, the defense team gets the ball and attacks the team waiting at the other end of the court.
4. Danyelle lets everyone know the offensive team is down by one.
5. She instructs the defensive team, without the offensive team's knowledge, to employ a person-to-person defense.

6. She instructs the offensive team to read the defense and call the appropriate play. Thus, she creates a game-like scenario where both teams are using tactical awareness and tactical decision-making skills to gain a competitive advantage.
7. The game is continuous, as Danyelle can instruct the defensive team waiting at one end of the court, while the other teams compete at the opposite end. Thus, mimicking a game situation where the coach instructs their defense during live play.

Beyond using the game-based approach, coaches will spend a portion of practice preparing for an upcoming opponent. To prepare for an upcoming opponent, coaches may use practice time to share a scouting report of the opposing team's offensive and defensive strategies, review the offensive and defensive tendencies of opponents with a game-based approach, or show video clips of the opposing team in other competitions. Based on the setting they work in, coaches need to be able to teach the appropriate tactical skills relative to their sport. Below is a checklist to help coaches prepare to teach tactical skills for competitive success in youth sport.

TEACHING TACTICAL SKILLS CHECKLIST
- Identify the rules of play that need to be taught.
- Identify situations in competition where athletes need tactical awareness.
- Identify which tactical skills need to be taught, relative to age level and competitive setting.
- Identify situations in competition where athletes need to make in-game decisions.
- Identify the types of drills or game-based activities needed to teach tactical skills in practice.

FEEDBACK
Another key teaching tool coaches can use in practices and competition is giving effective feedback to promote athlete learning. Effective feedback is informational, motivational, and reinforcing without creating dependency.[13,14]

Informational Feedback
To give quality feedback coaches want to provide athletes useful information for improving their performance that is not redundant.[15] For example,

telling basketball players they missed a shot is redundant, but telling players they may be able to sink more shots if they follow through on their shot would provide them with key information for improving performance. Coaches also want to consider ways they can augment their verbal feedback to help athletes see, hear, or feel how they might improve their technical performance. For example, a coach could video record each athlete performing a few shots and then watch the video together pointing out some key areas for improvement. However, it will be important for a coach not to overload athletes with too much technical feedback. One or two key areas that need improvement should be targeted. Further, coaches want to consider how they can help their athletes develop their own technical capabilities for improving their performance. Therefore, in watching a video of boxing out a player after a rebound the coach may want to ask athletes to describe what they did well, what could be improved, and how they might improve their technique. The athlete could then work on implementing the change in the next competition and during the next video session look at the improvement or strategize some additional adjustments.

Encouraging Feedback

In giving informational feedback, coaches may also want to tie this to encouraging feedback (e.g., "You got this."; "I know you can do this."). By providing encouraging feedback, coaches send the message to athletes that they believe they are capable of making the necessary changes. Coaches can also follow up after the athlete makes the correction (e.g., "Nice, I like how you added that follow through. Keep up the good work.") to remind athletes about the action they took and how it helped their performance, encouraging them to continue the action.

Reinforcing Feedback

As displayed in the previous section on demonstrations, coaches also use feedback to reinforce correct actions. In fact, some coaches and practitioners suggest a majority of feedback should reinforce correct action.[16] Further, it is important to reinforce the effort and improvement associated with this correct action (e.g., "AJ, I like that improvement I am seeing in your footwork during games. It has really helped your play during games. Keep working on this in practice.") rather than ability (e.g., "AJ, your footwork was so much better than the opponent. You just crushed them."). This will send the message to athletes that their actions (i.e., the effort), which is in their control, results in change versus their innate ability, which is not controllable and can reduce motivation.[17] A final important point about reinforcing correct action: is that it does not mean coaches ignore errors. They can still use informational feedback. However, it is also important for coaches to identify errors and build follow-up practice plans to address these errors without necessarily bringing them to the attention of the athlete.

Feedback That Avoids Overdependence

While not providing enough feedback can be detrimental to learning, providing ill-timed or too much feedback can also hinder learning. Coaches who provide feedback to athletes as soon as they make a mistake can interfere with the athletes' own intrinsic feedback that allows them to self-correct based on what they see and how it feels.[18] Therefore, when coaches are teaching new techniques and tactics, they want to have athletes attempt the task a few times before rushing to give feedback to allow them to self-correct. Coaches also want to avoid correcting an error every time it occurs (i.e., giving too much feedback) as athletes can come to rely on this feedback making it more difficult to successfully perform on their own. Coaches will also want to consider how guided feedback during games (e.g., calling every play during a game) can also limit the decision-making ability of athletes as they become reliant on the coach to make decisions for them rather than encouraging personal responsibility and accountability.

THE PRACTICE SESSION

In planning a well-developed practice session, coaches implement effective learning principles and teaching methods outlined in this chapter. Coaches also develop effective practice sessions when considering how they will teach in addition to what they will teach. Therefore, coaches will also want to consider implementing the following into planning each practice session:

- Clear practice objectives: Identify clear objectives for the practice and focus all practice activities on working toward achieving these objectives.
- Structure: Provide a consistent framework to each practice to provide a general rhythm to practice and increase efficiency. Ensure the practice session

is set up to reinforce points from a previous practice, align with the season plan, and provide reminders for feedback.

- Skill development: Every activity in practice should focus on developing one or more of the following skills: technical, tactical, physical, mental, or life skills aligned with the objectives.
- Instructional style: Consider the instructional style that will best accomplish the objectives and skills to be developed during the practice and will motivate athletes.
- Progression: The teaching of skills should follow a sequence that aligns with the developmental stage of each athlete. Plus, the progression and flow of the practice should be considered.
- Plan demonstrations and feedback: Make plans to provide effective demonstrations during practice and consider when feedback will be provided and what form it will take.
- Quick transitions: Keep time between drills short and keep athletes active throughout practice by designing drills with smaller groups and higher repetitions.
- Load challenge: Individualize complexity and expectations to each athlete to ensure they are challenged during practices.
- Opening/closing: Provide a consistent activity to start a practice session that may include reinforcing skill development from the previous practice, an overview of what skills will be taught in this practice, or setting the tone of the practice session. Finish practice with an activity to reinforce key teaching points from the practice session, provide feedback to the entire team on their skill progression, and end practice on a positive note.

IN ACTION

TRAINING AND EVALUATING THE COACH AS A TEACHER

To support and guide volunteers, we recommend that youth sports administrators adopt a four-step process to managing coaches—screening, training, evaluating, and holding them accountable. All four steps play a role when it comes to helping coaches improve as teachers of their sport. During the screening process, administrators review applications and interview potential coaches to get a feel for their experience, motives, abilities, and any preexisting coaching philosophies. Then, providing all coaches a consistent and quality training curriculum sets a standard and equips them with tools needed to teach a sport to kids. Once the season starts, ongoing evaluation of the coaches through informal and formal feedback channels—from parent surveys to observing practices— allows administrators to address areas in need of improvement. Perhaps a site visit to a coach's practice reveals the participants are spending too much time standing in lines. That coach would benefit from learning more drills to keep all athletes involved and active throughout practice. Accountability is key to ensuring that the individuals who have the privilege to coach children are fit for the role. A coach can be trained about things like the importance of exemplifying good sportsmanship and why players should be exposed to a variety of positions, but if he or she is not meeting expectations, then a solid accountability process helps administrators take action. Established procedures for reviewing complaints and disciplinary or improvement protocols sends a message to all coaches, parents, and participants about what kind of coaching is expected and what is simply not tolerated.

—Kate Nematollahi, director, education programs,
National Alliance for Youth Sports (NAYS)

COACH TIPS!
- Become familiar with the different instructional styles to implement as a coach.
- Implement the *Five-Step Approach* to provide demonstrations during practice.
- Implement the game-based approach in practice sessions.
- Design practice activities that incorporate tactical decision making.
- Provide informational feedback to improve athlete performance.

- Provide feedback to encourage and reinforce the teaching of technical and tactical skills.

COACH DEVELOPER TIPS!

- Periodically observe practices and provide coaches insight into how they can improve and diversify their instructional styles.
- Share strategies with coaches on giving effective demonstrations and have them practice with peer coaches to get feedback for improving their presentation.
- During a practice, tabulate the amount and type of feedback a coach uses during practice. Share the findings with the coach with suggestions for ways to improve the use of effective feedback.
- Create an opportunity for the coaches in the program to share ways they are using the game-based approach to help their athletes learn the sport.

9

To Coach Is to Assess

The key role of a coach is to help athletes develop through participation in sport. However, how do coaches know development occurs? By implementing effective assessment methods, coaches can see the improvements being made, make adjustments when athletes are not developing as expected, and encourage athletes to monitor their improvements over the course of the season. Assessments also provide coaches information to use in making decisions during the season, from deciding who makes the team to who will start in games or participate in competitions.

PLANNING TO ASSESS

Victoria is a high school field hockey coach. She is in her third year of coaching and struggling a bit with athlete development. Her athletes have fairly good stick skills, but their conditioning and game sense has not developed very well. This has resulted in a poor showing on the field and athletes feeling frustrated because they do not feel like they are improving. In fact, four of her players recently told her they did not plan to come back next season. She also has had several parents question her ability to make decisions related to playing time, often sharing that they did not believe she was playing the right team members during games and this is why the team was struggling.

Victoria sat down with her athletic director, Sarah, to talk about her struggles. Sarah suggested she consider more closely what she was doing in practice. Sarah asked her a series of questions:

1. How do you show athletes they are improving?
2. How do you identify what practice drills, activities, small-sided games, and so forth are improving performance and what ones are hindering performance?
3. What criteria do you use to decide your starters?

Victoria realized she did not really have good answers to these questions. Sarah encouraged her to plan some assessments for the fall season that would inform her of what is working, help players see where they are improving, and strengthen her decisions about who starts. To begin this process, coaches, like Victoria, plan for assessment by considering the what, how, who, and when of the assessment process.

What to Assess

The first consideration is what to assess. That is, what aspects of holistic development do coaches want to assess throughout the season? While there are many aspects of athlete performance that could be assessed (see table 9.1), the answer to this question will depend on the goals of the program and the purpose of the assessment. As noted in chapter 2, coaches develop their

Table 9.1. Assessment Categories

4 C's of Athlete Outcomes	Assessment Categories
Competence	• Skills/techniques • Tactics/strategies/decision making • Strength and conditioning (agility, balance, coordination, strength, power, endurance)
Confidence	• Mental states (e.g., anxiety, confidence, resilience) • Mental skills (e.g., goal setting, imagery, self-talk)
Connection	• Interpersonal skills (e.g., verbal communication, listening, conflict resolution)
Character	• Sport conduct (e.g., fair play, respect for officials) • Life skills (e.g., responsibility, leadership, teamwork, work ethic)

program goals by considering the core values and standards of performance they want to embed in daily practice. These values and standards would be what coaches assess. For instance, if the goal of a youth sport program is skill development, then conditioning or tactical strategies would not be assessed. Rather, the coach would assess the various sport and life skills being taught during the program. In addition to looking at a program's core values and standards of performance, coaches will also want to consider the purpose of the assessment. For example, a coach may have a different assessment focus during the selection process (e.g., assessing fitness levels, skills, and attitude versus understanding of tactical strategy) from when assessing athletes during practice to monitor improvement and make practice adjustments.

How to Assess

The next consideration is how to assess athletes. Coaches will need to consider how to assess the various aspects of athlete performance and development. Coaches have several options including observing or videoing athlete performance during practices or competition. By using video technology, coaches can assess the quality of an athletic skill or how well the team executes a play. In addition, coaches can conduct performance tests (e.g., running a test set during practice and assessing fitness levels) or collect statistics on competition performance. Regardless of the method, coaches will also want to decide how to measure athlete performance. In some instances this is fairly straightforward, such as measuring the amount of weight lifted, time ran, or the number of shots made on goal. However, other times this is a bit more difficult. For instance, assessing skills could involve each of the following:

- Create a checklist of all skills where the coach places a check and the date when the athlete demonstrates age-appropriate proficiency at the skill. For example, a youth swim coach would list all the strokes and turns for swimming and check when the athlete had demonstrated proficiency (see figure 9.1).
- Create a form with elements of each skill noted. For example, a tennis forehand could include racket grip, body sideways, racket back, step forward with front foot, level swing, and follow through. Also, periodically throughout the season, coaches could use a rating scale to note whether athletes demonstrate each element of the skill over a number of attempts at the skill (see table 9.2).

Swimming Evaluation Form for _____

This checklist lets you know how you are doing in your swimming. A check next to each element means you have achieved proficiency for your age group and the date notes when this was achieved during the season.

Front Crawl Checklist

Arm Stroke

_____ Fingertips enter first
_____ Hand enters 8-10 inches before complete extension in front of shoulders
_____ Hands catch water as pulls toward midline as arms go over the barrel
_____ Hand pushes back past waist during finish
_____ Elbow is high and leads recovery

Kick

_____ Kick from hips
_____ Bend knees slightly on downbeat and keep knee straight on upbeat

Body Position and Breathing

_____ Proper head position with good body alignment throughout stroke
_____ Head turns short distance to breathe

Flip Turn

_____ Correct positioning from wall
_____ Does not breathe into or out of turn
_____ Pulls hand down and uses core to flip feet with hands staying in place
_____ Immediately and strongly push off the wall rotating into position with good streamlining
_____ Strong dolphin kick out of turn
_____ Pullout begins just as ready to break surface

Backstroke Checklist

Arm Stroke

_____ Extended arm enter water with little finger of hand entering first
_____ Straight arm recovery
_____ Elbow begins to bend as arm moves forward, reaching maximum bend at the shoulder
_____ Opposition rhythm

Kick

_____ Kick from hips
_____ Use small kicks and make water boil

Body Position and Breathing

_____ Head is back with ears slightly under water
_____ Shoulders roll, while head remains stationary
_____ Breathing is controlled as in front crawl

Flip Turn

_____ Correct positioning from wall (counts strokes into wall)
_____ Pulls hand down and uses core to flip feet with hands staying in place
_____ Immediately and strongly push off the wall with good streamlining
_____ Strong dolphin kick out of turn
_____ Pullout begins just as ready to break surface

Breaststroke Checklist

Arm Stroke

_____ Hands move apart elbows bend and hands angle backward and outward (triangle motion)
_____ Pull does not go any farther than shoulder width
_____ Elbows collapse down during recover as hands come together and move forward

Breathing and Head Motion

_____ Inhales quickly when head and shoulders rise naturally as a result of the pull
_____ Exhales when head is under water

Kick

_____ Aim for a narrow kick, the knees should be no farther than hip width apart
_____ Ankles flex
_____ Snaps lower legs and feet together in a downward and outward arc to get whip-like action
_____ Legs extend fully as they come together

Body Position

_____ Streamlined and extended as possible during glide
_____ Coordination is pull, breathe, kick and glide

Turn

_____ Two hand touch
_____ One hand quickly moves away from wall while body rotates and hips/legs tuck and feet touch wall
_____ Strong push off with good streamlining
_____ Strong dolphin kick out of turn
_____ Completes underwater pullout and stroke begins as ready to break surface

Butterfly Checklist

Arm Stroke

_____ Arms enter water shoulder width apart, slightly bent with thumbs entering first
_____ Hands move down and out in Y shape motion with elbows high
_____ Hands slide and finish by side of body
_____ Elbows lead recovery and stay higher as arms swing through

Kick

_____ Kick from hips
_____ Keep legs together
_____ Kick twice for each stroke – once when arms enter and once when arms exit water

Breathing

_____ Lift or turn head to breathe every other stroke
_____ Quick head motion for breathing

Turn

_____ Two hand touch
_____ One hand quickly moves away from wall while body rotates and hips/legs tuck and feet touch wall
_____ Strong push off with good streamlining
_____ Strong dolphin kick out of turn
_____ Pullout begins just as ready to break surface

FIGURE 9.1
Swimming Evaluation Form

Table 9.2.   Tennis Forehand Checklist

	Always (seen for all ten attempts)	Often (seen at least seven times)	Sometimes (seen at least four or five times)	Rarely (seen less than three times)
Racket grip	☐	☐	☐	☐
Body sideways	☐	☐	☐	☐
Racket back	☐	☐	☐	☐
Step forward with front foot	☐	☐	☐	☐
Level swing	☐	☐	☐	☐
Follow through	☐	☐	☐	☐

- Create a rating scale to assess the quality of skill or attribute. For example, the checklist below measures confidence level on a scale from 0 to 100. In using this scale, athletes check their level of confidence; that is, how confident they are right now playing this sport.

Check In on Confidence Scale
- ☐ 0 percent confident (Not confident at all)
- ☐ 10 percent confident
- ☐ 20 percent confident
- ☐ 30 percent confident
- ☐ 40 percent confident
- ☐ 50 percent confident (Somewhat confident)
- ☐ 60 percent confident
- ☐ 70 percent confident
- ☐ 80 percent confident
- ☐ 90 percent confident
- ☐ 100 percent confident (Extremely confident)

With any of these methods, coaches measure, observe, and communicate with athletes in both formal and informal testing settings to get a sense of how the athletes are performing relative to each quality or criteria. This is where technology can be helpful, whether it be using video analysis software to assess skills or creating an online folder filled with the assessments used throughout the season coaches and athletes will complete.

Who Will Assess

The third consideration in developing an assessment is who will assess. It is often assumed coaches will do the assessment, but it is possible to have the athlete engage in the assessment process. Therefore, coaches want to consider the intent of the assessment to determine who might be the best person to complete the evaluation. During the selection process, the head and assistant coaches may be the best choice. However, during practices, coaches may ask athletes to assess one another on their skills. Further, it may be helpful to have athletes self-assess as discussed later in this chapter.

When to Assess

The final consideration is when to assess. Coaches will want to consider the time of the season as well as the frequency of the assessment. For example, if coaches want to demonstrate improvement over the course of the season, they will want to assess at the beginning and end of the season.

Coach Victoria's Assessment Development

When reflecting on her conversations with Sarah, Coach Victoria realizes that she really does assess her athletes a lot during practices and games, but it is not a well thought-out or planned process. With new information about the assessment planning process, as described in this chapter, Coach Victoria decides to implement a few formal assessments to better facilitate and communicate athlete development and be able to clearly communicate playing decisions.

Improving Practice Planning and Execution

To help her judge the effectiveness of her practices, Coach Victoria decides to implement some periodic fitness tests to assess agility (e.g., 505 agility test), speed (40-yard sprint test), and endurance (e.g., 20-meter shuttle run), which she will build into the conditioning part of her practice every three weeks. Additionally, she creates a checklist of key tactical aspects she wants to reinforce throughout the season based on the six core skills of field hockey: pass and receive on the move, ball control, goal scoring, off the ball movement, individual defense, and team defense.[1] She will then use the checklist to evaluate the team during a scrimmage in practice every three weeks. With the data from these assessments in hand, Victoria can make adjustments in her conditioning and instructional plans in practice, provide the team feedback about how they are doing (what is going well and what they still need to work on as a team), and motivate the team by setting a goal for where they want to be by the next testing day.

Demonstrating Athlete Development

To show athletes the progress they make through the season, Victoria will focus on conditioning and skills of each individual athlete. She will develop a set of fitness and skill assessments to use at the beginning and end of the season. She will assess endurance, speed, and agility using timed tests and measure strength using vertical jump, burpee, and core muscle-strength tests. She will assess a variety of skills, such as possession, elimination, goal scoring, work ethic, and confidence by filming the athletes during some drills and scrimmages and evaluating key elements of the skills to share with players. After the preseason test, she will meet with each athlete and share the data describing strengths and weaknesses. Together, they will develop two or three goals for the season to improve key areas of conditioning and skills. During practices, Coach Victoria can then be strategic about providing feedback to athletes to help them continue to work toward achieving their goals.

Improving Selection Processes

To be more systematic about choosing starters, Victoria decides she is going to list the top 5–10 qualities (physical, mental, character qualities) she will look for in midfielders, forwards, defenders, sweepers, and goalies. She will share these lists with the athletes and using a rating scale (5 = exhibits all the time to 1 = rarely exhibits) identify players who are ready to start for weekly games based on her other assessments and observations in practices and games.

As Coach Victoria rightfully noted, coaches are assessing their athletes on a regular basis with many of these assessment moments occurring automatically. The benefit of planned assessments is that it provides coaches with data they can use to be more intentional in planning and executing practices, be more strategic in providing feedback to athletes about their progress and be more transparent with athletes and their families about coaching decisions.

PROCESS-BASED GOALS

At Ellensburg High School, we encourage our coaches to set standards for performance and assess their athletes and team separately on their progress toward meeting the standard and not just simply assess if they met the standard or not. In one form or another, all athletic programs at Ellensburg High School have adopted the "process over outcome" approach to guiding their program. We promote that if you meet the goals and standards identified in the process, the outcomes will take care of themselves. To assess the process, our athletic programs are encouraged to record multiple process-based pieces of data that are specific to the goals and standards they have defined for their program. Once the athletes are aware of what is being measured, they will have immediate feedback on whether or not they made progress toward their goal or standard, thus increasing their motivation to meet those standards and/or achieve their goals. Additionally, once the identified process-based goals and standards are met, the program can easily identify other areas on which to base new goals or standards. In track and field, it could be a one-lap time standard; in baseball it could be the percentage of first-pitch strikes thrown; and in basketball it might be team and/ or individual turnovers. We have found that when coaches take this approach, our athletes focus less on the outcomes of their competitive endeavors and more on the process which allows them to perform in the present moment.

—Cole Kanyer, athletic director, Ellensburg High School (WA)

NURTURING ATHLETE SELF-ASSESSMENT

While coaches often initiate assessment of their athletes, a good skill coaches can teach athletes is to assess themselves. By engaging in the process of self-assessment, athletes not only take ownership over their own development but also become more knowledgeable of themselves and their understanding of the sport.[2] Listed here are a few ways coaches can promote self-assessment:

- During a small-sided game, a soccer coach can freeze play and ask athletes, "Why was the attacker able to get through and score?" Based on the athlete's response, the coach might follow up with, "Alright, how should we do it this time?" Finally, they can offer encouragement after the self-assessment and state, "Great idea! Let's give it a try."
- After a track event, an athlete approaches the coach for feedback. To encourage self-assessment the coach implements Pia Nilsson, Lynn Marriott, and Ron Sirak's (2005) Good-Better-How Method,[3] in which the coach asks the athlete the following three questions:

  1. What was good about your performance?
  2. What could you do better?
  3. How could you improve those things you need to do better?

Throughout the process, the coach may offer suggestions for the good and better as well as brainstorm with the athlete about some improvement strategies to implement in practice.

- During a volleyball practice, a coach just demonstrated to the athletes how to do the jump serve. As they practice in pairs, the coach provides each group a checklist of the four key steps for a jump serve. As one athlete is performing the jump serve three times, the second athlete is reviewing the checklist to determine what steps are being included and what steps are not. After the three serves, the athlete gives feedback and the athlete attempts another three serves with additional peer athlete feedback. The pair then switch roles.
- A swim coach has athlete goal-setting meetings and asks each athlete what goals they have for the season related to times, stroke development, and

mental skill use. The coach offers insights but lets the athlete direct the conversation and identify goals and strategies for achieving them.

- During a basketball halftime, the coach splits the team into groups of five, giving them a minute to identify one thing that went well in the first half and one thing that needs to be improved in the second half. Each group then shares in 30 seconds or less what went well. Then each group shares in 30 seconds or less what needs to be improved. The coach wraps up with ideas for moving into the second half.

IN ACTION

NURTURING ATHLETE SELF-ASSESSMENT

As a golf coach I can see my players have learned when they can accomplish two things. First, they can self-assess their swing to better understand their own golf swing. For example, I have one player who misses right. This summer we focused on why her swing was causing her to miss right. Now that she has figured out why she misses to the right, she no longer wonders why she misses it and can usually fix it herself. I only have to ask her what she needs to do and she makes the adjustment. The second way I know my athletes are learning is when they hit a bad shot, they are able to just move on from it. The hardest part of golf is not swinging the club, but the distance between the ears. Hitting a bad shot isn't fun. What is worse is letting that one shot effect the entire round. I know my athletes have learned when they can just say "oh well" and move forward to focus on the next shot. My one goal for them at the end of a tournament or a practice is to enjoy their round. If they can do that then they have really won the round.

—Janci Spoo, head golf coach, Hermiston High School (OR)

By providing multiple opportunities for athletes to engage in self-assessment, coaches help athletes play an active role in their own development. However, coaches are still guiding athletes and providing instruction and insight. While younger or less experienced athletes will need to be provided more directed and concrete self-assessment experiences, as athletes gain more experience and cognitive maturity coaches can involve them more in the decision-making process for their own development.

COACH TIPS!

- Review standards of practice to see how they align with how athletes are assessed.
- Take time to consider the what, how, who, and when of each assessment used during the season.
- Communicate with athletes how assessments are used to help them improve.
- Teach athletes how to assess their own progress and ways to improve in collaboration with the team and coach.
- Reflect upon assessment results to see how to improve practice sessions.

COACH DEVELOPER TIPS!

- Observe tryouts and talk with coaches about their assessment procedures.
- Provide coaches with a variety of options they can use to assess their athletes.
- Assist the coach in developing assessments for consistency across the program.
- Offer a workshop to help coaches learn how to encourage self-assessment among their athletes.
- Assess coaches' performance to help them see how they can improve their practice.

To Coach Is to Adapt

To adapt is to adjust or modify to various conditions.[1] This is the life of a coach, as no day is exactly the same. Coaches make adjustments based on their coaching context, competitive schedule, the evolving development of individual athletes and team dynamics, roster changes from season to season, changes to the rules of play, updates to best coaching practice, and more. Adapting to change is a key component of coaching and may be key to sustainability. Leon Megginson, a prolific writer and teacher in business management, remarked, "According to Darwin's *Origin of Species*, it is not the most intellectual of the species that survives; it is not the strongest that survives; but the species that survives is the one that is able best to adapt and adjust to the changing environment in which it finds itself."[2] Learning to adapt is critical for coaches to fulfill all aspects of their role while best meeting the needs of their athletes and their team.

SCENARIO: HELPING COACHES ADAPT

Elena Martinez leans out over the railing. From the balcony outside her office, she is afforded a full view of the youth baseball players below her working with coaches. Elena owns the Pitch, Hit, and Run Baseball-Softball Training Facility. Pitch, Hit, and Run is a private sport training facility where youth baseball and softball players, ages 9–18, can work with elite-level coaches to learn advanced baseball and softball skills for future competitive success in their sport. Elena played baseball as a youth and fastpitch softball in high school and college. She started as a coach, but when she had the financial opportunity to open an elite-level training facility, she jumped at it. She employs four full-time coaches and six part-time coaches to train the athletes at her facility. Athletes sign up to work individually with a coach. Thus, Elena knows that for the success of her business, it is important to ensure her coaching staff are properly trained on the current best coaching practices and they are able to adjust and adapt to the needs of each individual athlete to help them reach their full potential. Although Elena is not a trained coach developer, she assumes some of the duties of a coach developer by educating and working collaboratively with her coaches to ensure staff adapt to the individual needs of each athlete. To do this, Elena assists her coaches in developing self-awareness and the ability to use assessment to make adjustments.

WILLINGNESS TO ADAPT THROUGH SELF-AWARENESS

Self-awareness is simply how clearly we see ourselves. The view of ourselves includes knowing our values and goals, how we typically respond in situations, our strengths and weaknesses, and how we impact others.[3] Researcher Tasha Eurich examined people's self-awareness and found that while most people might believe they are self-aware, only about 10–15 percent actually are self-aware.[4] To build self-awareness, she first suggests people get feedback from trusted colleagues who can offer honest and constructive insight. For example, coaches could ask other coaches they trust the following questions:

- I think these are my strengths and weaknesses in coaching; what do you think?
- During games, I am typically calm and collected; is that what you see?
- My athletes say I am not listening to them, but I bend over backwards to accommodate their interests; don't you think so?
- When I yell at my athletes, it really motivates them; aren't they more motivated?

The second suggestion Eurich offers is to ask "what" rather than "why" questions. More specifically, reflecting on the future rather than the past.[5] Thus, the type of questions shifts to asking why this happened to what can be done moving forward. Here are some examples:

- The question of why did the practice not go well, becomes, "What can I do moving forward to make practice more engaging?"
- The question of why my periodization plan is not resulting in speed gains could become, "What do I need to do differently to improve athletes' speed?"
- Instead of asking why are my athletes not listening to me, I could ask, "What can I do to build their trust?"

By seeking feedback from trusted colleagues and asking "what" rather than "why" questions, coaches increase self-knowledge, recognize what they do not know, and identify productive actions for adapting to their environment.

Helping Coaches Adapt through Self-Awareness

In the scenario at Pitch, Hit, and Run, Elena could take an active approach to help each member of her coaching staff become more self-aware by pairing up members of her coaching staff for peer feedback. For example, Coach A would attend a training session offered by Coach B and observe Coach B working with an athlete. Following the training session, both Coach A and B would meet and discuss how the session went. Coach A could offer direct feedback and Coach B could ask specific questions of Coach A, such as "Do you think I need to offer more feedback when that athlete struggled to get into a balanced position to field the ball or was it good to just let him struggle through it?" To encourage this type of peer interaction, Elena might provide a one-page form for Coach A to use when observing Coach B to help him write down key points. Also, Elena could use a staff meeting to prepare her coaches on how the peer feedback sessions work and include instruction on how coaches can take constructive criticism. In addition, they could learn how to ask themselves "what" type questions instead of "why" type questions to further adapt their coaching practice.

Coaches can also direct themselves through self-awareness exercises. For instance, a parent-volunteer flag football coach could seek feedback from a more established parent volunteer flag football coach after the game by asking how she got her youth players to work together so well to run set plays. Then, when planning the next practice, the coach might ask herself, "What can I implement from my discussion with the opposing coach to help my athletes understand and run our set plays more effectively?"

IMPLEMENTING REFLECTIVE CONVERSATIONS

One of the hallmarks of an effective coach is the ability to reflect in and on action to evaluate how effectively the plan is being translated in practice. In this context, the purpose of reflecting in and on action is to establish how effectively the training designed is supporting, stretching, and challenging athletes. Novice coaches working in isolation might find this a difficult concept to master independently. As coach developers or mentors, we can help shine a spotlight on the coach's decision-making capabilities. This can be undertaken by facilitating a series of reflective conversations in and around the observation of coaching performance.

Reflective conversation 1: During this initial or prereflection conversation, there is the opportunity for the coach developer to "check and challenge" thinking and training design consideration so that the coach can visualize, anticipate, and edit the plan before moving into practice. It also gives the coach developer the opportunity to clearly establish the target coach behaviors to observe.

Observation of coaching performance: The observation itself should focus on the coach's performance and the athletes' response and the context in which everything takes place. The coach developer's role during the observation is to observe and record all information which is related to the target behavior, not make value judgements, capture personal comments or questions independently from the data collection tool, and not to intervene at all except if there are significant health and safety issues.

Reflective conversation 2: This is an opportunity for the coach to analyze and discuss the data collected during the observation. It is an opportunity for the coach to generate and then receive feedback about their coaching performance and the responses of the athletes. This should be started by asking the coach to restate their goals for the session, both theirs and the athletes. Then, relative to both sets of goals the coach describes "what went well." Their perceptions should be reinforced with the data and observations generated. The coach should have full access to the data collected during the observation and be given the opportunity to explore the data and discuss their thoughts and observations. The question, "What would be even better if?" is useful to explore what didn't work or go to plan. This process encourages coaches to adapt in ways that will meet both theirs and the athletes' goals.

—Sarah McQuade, coach developer, e.t.c coaching consultants

USING ASSESSMENT TO ADAPT

Assessments provide coaches information about individual athletes, the team, and opponents. Coaches use this information not only to show athletes how they are developing but to make decisions about training methods, practice sessions, and competitions (see chapter 9 for scenario on Coach Victoria where she uses these principles to make adaptations in her coaching). In the scenario at Pitch, Hit, and Run, Elena creates a series of assessments coaches use with athletes and discusses with the coaches how they can adapt their coaching based on the assessment results. Here are few examples:

- Elena has created assessment checklists for each of the major skills within baseball and softball. She encourages coaches to assess athletes when they arrive at the facility and works with coaches to identify drills and activities to improve the athlete's technique. Every few weeks athletes are reassessed and she meets with coaches to discuss how to adapt their instruction and training based on progress made by the athletes.
- Elena created a series of strength and conditioning assessments that athletes complete upon arrival. Using this information, she works with coaches to periodize training aligned with athletes' current conditioning level. Every six weeks coaches reassess the athlete's strength and conditioning levels and adapt training protocols based on insight provided from Elena.
- Elena sends coaches out to observe athletes in competitions to see their techniques and conditioning in action. Elena demonstrates to coaches how this information can be used to adapt drills and activities used in their training and also encourages partnering among coaches to create game-based approaches to improve skills within game-like scenarios.
- Elena encourages coaches to scout competition within their area to get a better sense of what techniques and strategies would make athletes at their facility more competitive against their opponents. These techniques and strategies are then shared among coaches and they brainstorm how best to incorporate them into training with their athletes.

Using assessments to adapt provides coaches with needed information to help individual athletes grow and develop. However, it is important for coaches and coach developers to remember that each individual athlete is on a personal developmental journey, which coaches need to consider when developing plans based on assessments.

ONE APPROACH TO BEING ADAPTABLE

When coaching athletes with physical and cognitive impairments, being adaptable is a critical skill. As a mentor to these athletes, I have the responsibility of helping them overcome the obstacles they face and find success. Many of my athletes have little, if any, prior experiences with team sports prior to joining my program and those that do often had experiences that were less than memorable. When an athlete faces a challenge in performing a skill or understanding a concept, I encourage them to be open minded and willing to try things in a different way. Sometimes, this means breaking the skill down to its most rudimentary form and completely starting over, while at other times it can be as simple as holding a bat or stick slightly differently or changing a pattern of footwork ever so slightly. Oftentimes, I give my athletes the analogy about the shortest distance between two points being a straight line, with my own spin. While that straight line oftentimes is the desired route, it doesn't always work for everyone, and frankly, it doesn't matter to me how the athlete gets from point A to B. Their "line" can be a zig-zag, semicircle, or a figure eight, as long as they work with me to find a way that works for them to complete the task or learn the skill. Their personal journey from one point to another, and their eventual individual success, allows for many valuable learning experiences about their unique abilities, as well as an opportunity to build trust in me while allowing us to develop a meaningful, lasting relationship with one another. Sometimes, an athlete will become preoccupied with their difficulties interfering with the success of the team. However, first I always do my best to redirect their focus to individual success, as their development of self-confidence and achieving individual success is vital in the process of achieving team success.

—Marcus Onsum, head coach,
Robbinsdale Robins Adapted Athletics (MN)

ADAPTING THROUGH STRATEGIC DECISION MAKING

Decision making is a skill that can be developed. The ability of coaches to make decisions is enhanced by past coaching experience, as they learn to recognize situations that occur on and off the field of play and make time to reflect on current practice[6] (see chapter 11). Coach educators and researchers John Lyle and Chris Cushion[7] describe three types of decision-making scenarios that coaches encounter that involve different levels of urgency to make a decision:

1. *Slower Deliberate Decision Making.* This is the purposeful planning aspect of coaching (see chapter 7) where coaches make decisions in regard to the upcoming season, daily practices, and offseason.
2. *Semi-Deliberative Decision Making.* These are the decisions made during practice sessions to adjust drills to achieve the desired teaching outcomes, decisions made during the intermission of an athletic competition, and decisions made in regard to how the coach interacts with athletes based on interpersonal interaction.
3. *Speedy Non-Deliberative Decision Making.* These are decisions coaches have to make as athletes are engaged in competitive play.

Although coaches use all three types of decision making, the following example focuses on the development of strategic decisions during competitions (i.e., semi-deliberative or speedy non-deliberative decision making) to give their athletes the best chance at competitive success.

Mi-Sook, a middle school girls' basketball coach, might employ strategic decision making in action (i.e., speedy non-deliberative). For example, during the second quarter of the contest, the opposing team switches their offensive style of play to account for their size advantage on the court. The offensive team has placed their tallest player on the low block, near the basket, and their second tallest player at the high post, near the free throw line. They are using a high-low exchange with the two players as an offensive strategy. Mi-Sook's team, which is a bit on the shorter side in height for a basketball team, faced a similar situation earlier in the season. Since she now recognizes the situation and because she has made adjustments in practice to prepare for this scenario, if it were to happen again, she is ready. Mi-Sook calls to her team to switch their defense to a person-to-person style and to front the low post player, with help from the defense on the weak side of the court, away from the ball. Her decision in this instance was quick and in the moment, or speedy and non-deliberative.

In the same contest, Mi-Sook's team heads into halftime down five points. Her team manager hands her a stat sheet. Mi-Sook notices her team is getting out rebounded and is giving up quite a few offensive boards. Knowing this she matched certain athletes to defend opposing players, Mi-Sook makes note of which player on the opposing team is getting the most offensive rebounds. Based on this information, she makes the adjustment at halftime to have a different player on her team defend this particular player. Since there is a pause in action (halftime intermission), Mi-Sook was able to employ a more semi-deliberative decision-making approach.

To make effective decisions, it is important coaches align their decision making with their purpose as a coach (see chapter 1) and their coaching philosophy (chapter 2). Further, coaches' decision-making efforts are improved when they critically evaluate when change is necessary. To assist in these endeavors, coaches want to ask themselves the following questions when considering adjustments:

- Is the change consistent with my coaching philosophy and the core values of the program? Or is it time to change philosophy and core values?
- Will the change build on the strengths of the team or individual athletes, or am I blindly adopting a scheme that may not work for my coaching context or athletes?
- Have I sought out feedback from trusted colleagues, athletes, and administrators to inform changes? Have I been open to the feedback provided?
- Am I making changes based on data (observations, assessments, statistics, research, etc.)? Do I know what is working and what is not working? Am I considering the evidence or understanding the rationale for making a change?
- Have I given myself enough time to develop or institute a plan with my athletes before making further changes?
- Is this the most critical change that needs to happen right now?

Over time, the ability of coaches to make effective decisions will likely determine their longevity as a coach, as decision making is a key component of being able to adapt as a coach.

CONCLUSION

In working with athletes, coaches adjust their training methods, instructional approach, and competition plan at any moment. The ability to successfully adapt occurs when coaches become self-aware and use information from a variety of sources (assessments, previous experiences, and learnings from others), as well as develop decision-making skills. This chapter provided some initial insight into how coaches can better adapt to their ever-changing environments. Additionally, the following tips might help coaches and coach developers in their journey toward making adaptations in their programs.

COACH TIPS!

- Develop self-awareness through reflection, honest conversations with trusted mentors, and moving from "why" to "what" questions.
- Consider how to effectively use assessments and other key pieces of information to make updates in training and competitive readiness.
- Communicate with others and observe other coaches to learn more about the sport to make better decisions during competitive events.

COACH DEVELOPER TIPS!

- Provide coaches resources for improving self-awareness.
- Meet with coaches to introduce reflective questions to encourage further self-awareness.
- Ask coaches to share how they are updating and adapting practice sessions and training methods based on assessments and other information gathered during the season.
- Observe the decision making of coaches during competitive play and discuss with the coach ways to improve semi-deliberative and speedy non-deliberative decision making.

11

To Coach Is to Get Better Every Day

Under the guidance of coaches, athletes continue to improve their physical, social, and mental skills. Becoming a more effective coach occurs when coaches are striving to improve their own professional, interpersonal, and intrapersonal knowledge to become a more effective coach.[1] Each day is an opportunity for coaches to get better at their craft. This occurs when coaches can engage in self-reflection and build support networks to better evaluate their own performance and stay up-to-date on the latest information to improve their effectiveness as a coach.

COACH WASHINGTON'S DILEMMA

Coach Washington slumped into the metal folding chair, his elbows rested mid-thigh, steadying his cupped hands around his face. Water slapped the marble floor tile in the shower room next to the tiny closet made into a coach's office. Noise from the shower room filtered through, rising a bit as Coach Robbins, his assistant coach, opened the door and entered the office. He noticed the dejected look on Coach Washington's face.

"You alright coach?" asked Coach Robbins. "That was a great win today! Did something happen?"

"Yeah, we won alright," quipped Coach Washington. "But this team has no fire, no passion, they just don't seem to like the game enough. I really do not feel like I can connect with them."

Coach Robbins said nothing. He could tell it was just best to let Coach Washington keep going. Coach Washington continued, "Remember that team we had five years ago? How much they loved to play and loved to play together? I want to recapture that with this team."

Coach Robbins nodded, expecting Coach Washington to continue. He was not really sure why he was so down on this team. The high school varsity team was 9–1. The athletes responded to coaching and they had some very talented players. They also respected Coach Washington. He had built quite a reputation in his five years as head coach and had won more than 80 percent of his games. When Coach Washington remained silent, Coach Robbins decided the coast was clear and said, "That was a great team we had in your first year, Coach, but this is a different team and they are good in different ways."

"Then why am I not having any fun coaching them?" he blurted back, in a lower tone to avoid being overheard. "I mean, the system we use has proven to be successful each year, we have improved the efficiency of how we run practice, and we even implemented a team retreat this season.

"They just don't like the game enough for me," he continued a little bit more agitated about his inability to share his passion with this group.

Again, Coach Robbins just nodded, unsure what else he could say.

Finally, Coach Washington threw up his hands and at the same time stating, "How can they not love this game?"

Questions to Consider

There are a lot of reasons why Coach Washington might be struggling in his role as a coach, one of which may have to do with his prior preparation to be a coach or his ability to keep learning as a coach. Take a moment to consider this scenario in more detail by responding to the following questions. The situation involving Coach Washington will be revisited at the end of the chapter.

1. What might be the reason for Coach Washington's disappointment in his team's lack of passion for the game?
2. Is there something missing in Coach Washington's development as a coach that is hindering his ability to deal with this situation?
3. Is Coach Washington being too hard on himself?
4. Does this situation reflect on his ability as a coach?

DEVELOPING AS A COACH

Due to the number of volunteer youth sport coaches in community sport programs, some coaches may have no background in youth sport, having never participated as an athlete. Others may have played youth sport, but have no training as a coach other than the coach orientation meeting prior to the season and/or a coaching principles class they enrolled in during college. Youth coaches more interested in coaching competitively at the club or scholastic sport level may have pursued additional coursework and either earned certification or an undergraduate degree (minor or major) in coaching. Lastly, either based on their own interest or as directed by a sport organization, coaches may acquire certification relative to a specific sport.

Whether or not youth sport coaches are trained, they will still do most of their learning on the job. Hands-on learning is one of the key characteristics of learning how to coach, as it is during coaching practice that coaches can apply the concepts learned in previous training. Jean Côté and Wade Gilbert[2] (2009) identified three types of knowledge coaches acquire to be an effective coach: professional, intrapersonal, and interpersonal knowledge.

- Professional knowledge is understanding how to coach. This is the knowledge relative to the coach's specific sport (i.e., technical and tactical skills), in addition to the general knowledge of the roles and responsibilities of a coach.
- Intrapersonal knowledge is understanding who you are as a coach. This is the ability to reflect continuously on current practice as a coach and make adjustments accordingly for long-term development.
- Interpersonal knowledge is understanding how to work with others. This is the knowledge of how to communicate and interact with all stakeholders relative to the setting the coach works in.

Coaches use a variety of formal, nonformal, and informal learning experiences to acquire the above requisite knowledge to be an effective coach. The following are common methods for developing as a coach:[3]

- Formal learning: A structured setting designed around learning outcomes and/or verification of completion (certification or degree), facilitated by an individual (e.g., instructor, supervisor, or manager).

- ○ A university course or degree program
- ○ Online training program
- ○ An ongoing coach development program (e.g., curriculum based)

- ▪ Nonformal learning: A short-term organized setting designed to encourage self-directed learning that is facilitated by an instructor and/or the coaches themselves.

- ○ Weekend workshop
- ○ Coaching clinic
- ○ Coaching convention

- ▪ Informal learning: Self-directed learning activities initiated by the coach using a variety of resources, which includes on-the-job training.

- ○ Online videos (e.g., YouTube or CoachTube)
- ○ Informal conversations with other coaches
- ○ Trial and error in practice sessions
- ○ Observation of other coaches

Youth sport coaches can engage in a variety of learning experiences to improve their knowledge for best coaching practice. But the most important action coaches can take is to strive to get better every day. Three actions to help in this endeavor are participating in self-reflection, engaging in self-directed learning, and developing support networks.

DAILY SELF-REFLECTION

Coaches are constantly reflecting on their coaching practice. They think about the effectiveness of a new drill they tried in practice or how well the substitution pattern worked in the most recent athletic contest. After a game or contest, they evaluate individual player and team performance, reflect on an exchange with a referee, and assess their ability to prepare a competitive strategy. Coaches also reflect on the past season, often in regard to how the athletes progressed in their ability to perform technical and tactical skills. While coaches take time to reflect on a practice session or contest, is the action deliberate or not? In other words, are they using specific reflection activities to improve coaching practice?

Reflective practice is a process that requires practitioners to stop and consider how they can improve current practice.[4] Thus, reflective practice activities are used to enhance personal and professional growth across all professional fields.[5] For coaches, reflective practice is a deliberate action to pause and consider coaching practice.[6] According to Wade Gilbert and Pierre Trudel[7] (2001), reflective practice for a coach can occur in three different ways. First, reflection occurs in action; for example, during a live competition or a live practice session. Second, the coach reflects on action; in other words, during a pause in competition or a break during a training session. Lastly, the coach engages in retrospective-on-action, which is reflection between competitions, practice sessions, or during the offseason.

Table 11.1 highlights five reflective practice activities with an example of how coaches can apply each for long-term growth and development: reflective journaling, reflective conversation, R-cards, think aloud, and personal narrative.[8]

Reflective practice activities can range from simple to more complex. For example, a simple reflection exercise would be a coach taking two minutes in the morning to reflect on yesterday's practice and decide the focus for today's practice. A more complex example would be reflective journaling as described in table 11.1. Whether coaches use simple or complex reflective-practice activities, the most important step coaches can take to implement reflective-practice activities in their ongoing development is to set aside specific time for reflection. For example, five to ten minutes after practice, five to ten minutes after competition, and a couple of hours at the conclusion of the season. During these short reflection sessions, coaches can ask themselves a series of questions to focus their reflection and make good use of their time. The list below provides an example of questions youth coaches can ask themselves postpractice, postcompetition, and postseason.

Postpractice
1. What went well during practice today?
2. What can we improve on for the next practice?
3. In what areas was I not prepared for as a coach?
4. How can I be more prepared for the next practice?

Table 11.1. Reflective Practice Activities

Reflective Activity	Description	Application in Practice
Reflective journaling	Coaches document their thoughts and actions over a period of time to adjust and enhance coaching practice.[1]	At the end of each practice session and prior to planning the next practice session, the coach takes 15 minutes to document her thoughts (written text or voice transcription) using either a series of predetermined self-reflection questions or categories (e.g., defense, hustle, motivation) to guide his or her response.
Reflective conversation	A deliberate action by coaches to construct knowledge through meaningful learning experiences using an ongoing process that facilitates the identification of coaching issues and then generates strategies to achieve the desired outcome.[2]	During the offseason, the coach identifies that his or her team peaks too early during the season. He or she takes action by speaking with successful coaches to develop strategies to implement with his team the next season. After experimenting with the new strategy, the coach repeats the reflective process by evaluating how the strategy worked and continues the process until he or she is satisfied with how the team finishes the season.
R-cards	Coaches record their thoughts during a practice session or contest (i.e., in action) using a predetermined checklist and then revisit the checklist and reflect (i.e., on action) on what they have learned.[3]	During a practice session, when the coach recognizes something he or she wants to reflect on in more detail later, she briefly removes herself from coaching practice (e.g., 15 seconds) and documents the item or issue on a predetermined checklist. Then after the practice session, he or she reviews the checklists and reflects on how to improve coaching practice using either a series of predetermined self-reflection questions or a record sheet.
Think aloud	Coaches verbalize their thoughts during a practice session or contest using an audio recording device.[4]	During a practice session, the coach provides instruction and then briefly (e.g., 30 seconds) removes herself from coaching practice and speaks out loud what she is thinking at that moment. She captures a recording of her voice using an audio recording application on her smartphone.
Personal narrative	Coaches share their coaching journey, both personal and professional, with a coach developer through interviews, written text, or both.[5]	During the offseason, the coach schedules a time to meet with a coach developer and through a recorded conversation/interview, she shares her personal story as it relates to coaching. Either through self-reflection or with the assistance of the coach developer, he or she can analyze how her personal story has influenced or continues to influence her development as a coach.

Sources:
1. Jennifer A. Moon, *A Handbook of Reflective and Experiential Learning: Theory and Practice* (New York: Routledge, 2013).
2. Clayton R. Kuklick and Michael Kasales, "Reflective Practice to Enhance Coach Development and Practice," in *Coach Education and Development in Sport: Instructional Strategies*, ed. Bettina Callary and Brian Gearity (New York: Routledge, 2019), 76–77.
3. Ceri Hughes, Sarah Lee, and Gavin Chesterfield, "Innovation in Sports Coaching: The Implementation of Reflective Cards," *Reflective Practice* 10, no. 3 (2009): 367–84, https://doi.org/10.1080/14623940903034895.
4. Amy Whitehead, Brendan Cropley, Tabo Huntley, Andy Miles, Laura Quayle, and Zoe Knowles, "Think Aloud: Toward a Framework to Facilitate Reflective Practice amongst Rugby League Coaches," *International Sport Coaching Journal* 3, no. 3 (2016): 269–86, https://doi.org/10.1123/iscj.2016-0021.
5. Brian T. Gearity, "Autoethnography," in *Research Methods in Sport Coaching*, ed. Lee Nelson, Ryan Groom, and Paul Potrac (New York: Routledge, 2014), 205–16.

Postcompetition

1. How were we prepared to compete today?
2. How can we improve our preparation for competition?
3. How well did we execute the game plan?
4. How well did we represent ourselves, the team, and the program during competition?

Postseason

1. Did we achieve our desired outcomes this season?
2. What do I need to improve on to ensure we meet desired outcomes next season?
3. In what areas did the athletes improve the most this past season?
4. In what areas did the athletes fail to improve during this past season.

Coach Washington and Self-Reflection

Following the competition, Coach Washington is frustrated about what he perceives is a lack of passion by his athletes. They do not seem to enjoy playing the game. He can tell, because he remembers how much he loved playing the game. He would arrive early on game days just to sit and look at the field and get mentally prepared to compete. He was always ready in the locker room before the game, his eyes focused on the coach, attentive to the message being shared in the pregame speech. On the field, he always gave his best effort, regardless of the score. While he wanted to please his coach, more important, he wanted to do his best, because to him there was a lot of joy in playing well. Coach Washington did not get the same sense from his athletes. They seemed to be motivated more by his actions than by their own, and his passion for the game could only carry them so far. They needed to have it.

While he is reflecting postcompetition, Coach Washington's approach could limit his ability to utilize this reflective time to improve team and/or coaching performance. He could take a more deliberate approach and implement a series of self-reflection questions or employ one or more of the reflective practice activities (see table 11.1). For example, if Coach Washington utilized the self-reflection questions, he might be able to keep his focus more on his athlete's performance and ability to implement the game plan during competition and be less critical of their lack of passion compared to his. For long-term coach development, Coach Washington could engage in reflective journaling to better document how he is improving his coaching practice and engage in reflective conversations with other coaches to overcome his limitations as a coach. Coach Washington's frustration with his team's lack of passion might be rooted in his own fading passion for the game he loves. By having better self-awareness of his coaching practice through reflective-practice activities, Coach Washington will be better equipped to deal with his frustration as a coach and recognize how it may be impacting his ability to adequately evaluate the performance of his team. Furthermore, through self-reflection activities, he may realize that he needs to do more to increase their passion, as he has discovered he is hindering it. To learn what to do next, Coach Washington might engage in self-directed learning activities.

SELF-DIRECTED LEARNING

The ongoing development of coaches is predicated on their ability to be self-directed learners. Self-directed learning is where the learner takes ownership of the learning process, enacting autonomy for what type of material they seek to learn and in what format they prefer to learn the new concepts.[9] In order for self-directed learning to be effective, coaches must take ownership of the learning process through their desire to learn and interest in getting better as a coach. In addition, they must learn how to apply new learning to current coaching practice and be able to reflect on their progress.[10]

Self-directed learning aligns with the coach development opportunities available to coaches. For example, if youth coaches attend a local coaching clinic, they may learn a new defensive strategy to apply with their team for the upcoming season. However, the information they received may have only introduced them to the topic and they need more information to apply the concepts in practice. Therefore, youth coaches could engage in a variety of learning experiences to further expand their knowledge on this topic; for example, self-paced online courses, self-study using online videos posted by other coaches (e.g., YouTube or CoachTube), books, or online resources (e.g., instructional guides) posted by sport organizations.

One of the challenges of self-directed learning is knowing where to look for information. For youth coaches there are several types of organizations or institutions that provide coaching resources. They include coaching associations (e.g., National Fastpitch Coaches Association), nonprofit sport organizations (e.g., National Alliance for Youth Sport, Positive Coaching Alliance), higher education (e.g., degree programs), national governing bodies of sport (e.g., USA Swimming), and for-profit organizations or businesses (e.g., 3D Institute, Athlete Assessments).

Coach Washington and Self-Directed Learning

If Coach Washington has a desire to improve as a coach, then he could start to implement self-directed learning concepts by taking the following steps:

1. Connect with the organizations and/or coaching associations that oversee his sport to access resources and/or participate in coaching clinics to grow his professional knowledge.
2. Reflect on areas that he would like to improve on as a coach.
3. Engage in self-study on one of the areas he wants to improve on by attending sessions at a coaching clinic/workshop and/or by accessing resources on the topic.
4. Using an already established support network, reach out to members of the network and seek their assistance/advice on how best to implement the new ideas in coaching practice.
5. Apply the new learning in an upcoming practice or training session.
6. Engage in reflective practice activities to evaluate the effectiveness of implementing the new learning and make adjustments as needed.
7. Include self-directed learning as part of an ongoing coach development plan.

SUPPORT NETWORKS

It can be difficult for coaches to navigate youth sport coaching on their own. Therefore, it is important that coaches build a support system, a group of coaches and/or professionals to help support them in their development as a coach. There are three specific steps coaches can take to connect with other coaches for support: meeting and getting to know coaches, collaborating and working with coaches in their network, and nurturing relationships with coaches for long-term support.[11]

1. *Meeting and getting to know coaches.* In order to build a support network, coaches need to go where the coaches are. This includes local, regional, and national coaching clinics; sport-specific national coaching conventions (e.g., American Football Coaches Association National Convention); local

and regional youth tournaments in the sport they coach (e.g., high school state championships); face-to-face, university-based coaching courses; live training workshops; working sport camps; and attending practices or training sessions conducted by effective coaches. In addition, coaches, if working as teachers in a K–12 setting, can work with their administrator to utilize in-service days to attend coaching conferences and meet other coaches. Also, coaches can connect with other coaches in their school or school district during already scheduled professional development time established by the athletic director for coach development.

2. *Collaborating and working with coaches.* Once coaches make a connection, they can continue to grow their network by demonstrating competence in their ability to communicate, listen, and keep their word. For example, a volunteer youth hockey coach may reach out to a scholastic hockey coach she met at a coaching clinic and volunteer to work her fundamental skills camp this coming summer. If the scholastic coach offers her a spot working the camp, the volunteer coach would need to demonstrate competence and responsibility in being prepared to teach basic fundamental skills, follow through on her commitment to working the camp, and be on time for camp each day.

3. *Nurturing relationships.* Having made a connection with a coach (step 1) and spent time working with the coach (step 2), coaches can further enhance the relationship by establishing a communication system (e.g., text messaging, phone calls, handwritten notes) to keep in touch, reach out to coaches to celebrate recent accomplishments, and seek guidance to nurture potential mentor-mentee relationships. Using the example of the volunteer youth hockey coach, after working the summer camp the volunteer coach could stay in touch with the scholastic coach throughout the year via email, reach out and congratulate the coach on a great win during the season, and occasionally ask for advice on how to best teach a hockey skill or implement a defensive strategy for her youth team.

In addition to utilizing the three steps, the impact of having a support network can be greatly enhanced by participating in a community of practice.

Community of Practice

In sport coaching, a community of practice (CoP) is a group of coaches that share an identity (e.g., scholastic coaches) and have a desire to improve their knowledge (e.g., coaching practice) by interacting with one another on a consistent basis.[12] Coaches can join an already established CoP or form their own. In creating a CoP, youth coaches should consider reaching out to coaches that share commonalities, such as coaching in the same context or coaches facing similar challenges. In addition, youth coaches need to consider how members of the CoP will interact with one another, what each member can bring to the group, and who might be best to facilitate sessions for the CoP.

When joining an already established CoP, youth coaches look for a group of coaches that reinforce their coaching philosophy while also challenging them to grow and develop. Often CoPs naturally form among coaches in specific sports. One example of a naturally formed CoP is the Snow Valley Basketball Camps (SV). Since 1960, SV has created an environment for coaches to learn and develop as coaches while they are engaged in coaching practice (i.e., teaching basketball skills to youth athletes attending the camp).[13]

While SV is not a formally structured CoP, it provides basketball coaches three key components of a successful CoP, which are reflect, share, and create knowledge.[14] SV is structured around the teaching of basketball skills through instructional clinics. In an instructional clinic, one coach will serve as a lead coach. The task of the lead coach is to facilitate the teaching of the basketball skill and provide a demonstration of the drill that will be used to practice the skill. The lead coach will be joined by a number of assistant coaches who will observe the lead who is teaching the skill. After the lead has finished providing instruction, the assistant coaches will implement the drill at a number of baskets, providing feedback, and instruction to the youth practicing the skill. Once the session is over, the lead coach along with the assistant coaches can convene and evaluate how the session went. The lead might receive direct feedback from the assistant coaches, or the assistant coaches might ask questions of the lead for clarification. In this environment, the lead coach could be either a veteran or novice coach. In other words, a more experienced coach might be serving in the role of an assistant and can provide valuable feedback to a novice coach leading the clinic. The instructional clinic operates like a CoP because SV provides a setting where coaches reflect, share, and create knowledge.

In addition to the instructional clinics, SV provides a setting where different coaches with varying expertise can facilitate informal coaching clinics with a small group of coaches. These informal sessions occur late at night and into the early morning hours or during meal breaks of the overnight camp, anytime the coaches are not engaged with the youth participants. Similar to instructional clinics, the informal clinics operate much like a CoP because coaches can share and create knowledge, often being facilitated by a more knowledgeable coach on the topic being discussed.

Lastly, because coaches work closely together over a five-day period and share a similar passion for teaching the game of basketball, there is a natural inclination to form strong bonds with the other coaches working the camp. This bond provides each coach ongoing support well after the camp has finished; a network of coaches to help each other overcome common challenges and celebrate each other's success. This ongoing connection with other coaches follows the makeup of an effective CoP as coaches return to coaching practice implementing ideas they learned from their involvement in SV. Then through reflection on implementation and in continued conversation with the CoP, they improve coach practice over time. The importance of forming support networks for long-term growth and development can be accomplished by meeting new coaches, working with and nurturing relationships with coaches in their network, and being involved with a CoP.

CONCLUSION

By identifying self-directed learning opportunities, reaching out to seek the support of others, and engaging in reflective practices on a regular basis, coaches improve their craft in multiple ways that are unique to them. In the two in-action examples below, see how one coach describes his journey toward continual improvement and how a coach developer guides coaches on their journey.

IN ACTION

ONE COACH'S ONGOING DEVELOPMENT JOURNEY

To be a better coach, one must commit to personal growth as well as growth as a coach. To keep my personal identity as a coach healthy, I typically seek to read a book based on a concept or topic in which I would like to learn or grow. This reading enables me to reflect upon my personal values, which drive my reasoning. As a coach, I strive to learn from others, often across geographic areas and in other sports. Each year, I try to visit established athletic programs in various states and attend all of their team meetings, practices, and games for one week. I try to learn about their culture, find unique aspects of their daily operations, and discuss the strategic and technical details of their program. From those experiences, I get a chance to reassess my program and use any new information to improve our current culture and approach. In addition, I believe that planning and preparation are vital to improve as a coach. I typically assess proficiency and efficiency prior to leaving the practice facility. Proficiency refers to achieving the goal of the activity, while efficiency refers to using the assigned time in the proper manner. Such reflection enables me as a coach to make improvements and changes to achieve the goal, strategically and technically. Following a review of the practice plan, I spend ten minutes reflecting upon my interactions in practice using my established personal values. Such values guide my interactions with the athletes. If my actions do not honor my values, I write down one to two principled statements that help guide my interactions the following day.

—Marcis Fennell, head football coach, Seattle, WA

IN ACTION

HELPING COACHES ON THEIR DEVELOPMENTAL JOURNEY

To help a coach is to know a coach. Before I can help, I have to know their current aptitude, motivation, and determination. I have to know their current situation, not only professionally,

(continued)

HELPING COACHES ON THEIR
DEVELOPMENTAL JOURNEY (continued)

but, more important, personally. Where are they and where do
they want to go? What do they need to learn to get where they
want to go and what plan can they develop to achieve their goal?
Are they pursuing coaching as a career, as a hobby, as a way
to give back to their community? Like any nonlinear endeavor,
things change. Goals change, people change, situations change,
opportunities come and go. Life happens. So reflection is critical, especially during times of change, providing evaluation and
insight. Evidence confirms coaches are not very self-aware of
their abilities. A reality-based assessment of current capabilities
requires a baseline assessment to compare those capabilities to
the skills necessary to achieve their desired level of craftsman-
ship. Once a baseline assessment is complete, they can develop a
plan, which like anything else, will change. Many coaches initially
think the coaching craft solely involves the Xs and Os in practice
and games, but the art of coaching exists in building meaningful
relationships. Coach development is no different. Just like player
development, coach development is people development. And to
develop the person, I must know the person.

—Matt Dacey, national instructor, US Soccer

COACH TIPS!

- Incorporate a daily or weekly coach reflection plan to reflect upon how
  practices are going, to celebrate success, and look for opportunities to improve the structure of practice.
- Reflect upon strengths and weaknesses to determine knowledge gaps. Identify a variety of self-directed learning activities to fill those gaps.
- Look for opportunities to network with coaches to seek and share advice.
- Create or join a community of practice.

COACH DEVELOPER TIPS!

- Model the reflective process by observing a coach using formative evaluation tools or targeted assessments to identify strengths and weaknesses of coaching practice, share the findings, and discuss ways to improve practice, identifying one or two things to apply in practice. Follow up to see how it went.
- Share with the coach the reflective practice process and how it can improve coaching practice.
- Talk with the coach to outline strengths and weaknesses along with areas of improvement.
- Assist the coach in identifying ways to improve coaching practice through formal and informal learning experiences.
- Provide opportunities for coaches to work with and talk to one another. Even consider initiating a community of practice or mentoring program with the coaches in the program.

Appendix

Resources for Keeping Athletes Safe

ESTABLISHING AND MANAGING A RESPECTFUL ENVIRONMENT

Bystander Revolution's Example of Bystander Intervening When Bullying Occurs: https://www.bystanderrevolution.org/v/Shereen+%7C+Keep+the+Athletes+In+Check/opLugXo87bY

Child Welfare Information Gateway Lists State Reporting Mandates: https://www.childwelfare.gov/topics/systemwide/laws-policies/statutes/manda/

International Olympic Committee's Scenarios on Creating a Harassment Free Environment: https://www.olympic.org/sha

PACER's Bully National Prevention Center: https://www.pacer.org/bullying/classroom/planet-fitness/

Play Like a Champion Today, Bullying Resources: https://www.playlikeachampion.org/bullying

StopBullying.Gov Lists State Laws on Bullying and Hazing: https://www.stopbullying.gov/resources/laws/key-components

StopBullying.Gov Resources on Ways to Encourage Bystanders to Act Against Bullying: https://www.stopbullying.gov/prevention/bystanders-to-bullying

US Center for SafeSport Parent Toolkit: https://uscenterforsafesport.org/wp-content/uploads/2020/05/Parent-Toolkit_Complete-1.pdf

US Center for SafeSport Training: https://safesport.org/

USING SAFE TRAINING PRACTICES

Concussion Training: https://nfhslearn.com/courses/61064/concussion-in-sports; https://www.cdc.gov/headsup/highschoolsports/training/

CPR and First Aid Training: https://www.redcross.org/take-a-class

National Alliance for Youth Sport Emergency Action Plan Template: https://www
.nays.org/default/assets/File/Emergency%20Action%20Plan%20Template.pdf

National Athletic Trainers' Association Emergency Action Plan White Paper:
https://www.nata.org/sites/default/files/white-paper-emergency-action-plan.pdf

National Athletic Trainers' Association Position Statement: Environmental Cold
Injuries: https://europepmc.org/article/med/19030143

National Athletic Trainers' Association Position Statement: Exertional Heat
Illnesses: https://meridian.allenpress.com/jat/article/50/9/986/112280/National
-Athletic-Trainers-Association-Position

National Athletic Trainers' Association Position Statement: Lightning
Safety for Athletics and Recreation: https://meridian.allenpress.com/jat/
article/48/2/258/111337/National-Athletic-Trainers-Association-Position

National Athletic Trainer's Association's Hydration Guidelines: https://www.nata
.org/sites/default/files/healthy-hydration-for-young-athletes.pdf

National Athletic Training Association and the North American Booster Club
Association Sports Safety Checklist: https://www.nata.org/sites/default/files/
sports-safety-checklist.pdf

National Eating Disorders Association's Coaches & Trainer Toolkit: https://www
.nationaleatingdisorders.org/sites/default/files/Toolkits/CoachandTrainerTool
kit.pdf

National Youth Sports Health & Safety Institute: Optimal Nutrition for Youth
Athletes: http://nyshsi.org/wp-content/uploads/2012/08/NYSHSI-Optimal
-Nutrition-for-Youth-Athletes.pdf

Safe Kids' Sport Safety Checklist for Coaches: https://www.safekids.org/sites/default/
files/documents/sports_safety_checklist_for_coaches.pdf

Stop Sports Injuries, Coaches' Resources: https://www.stopsportsinjuries.org/STOP/
Prevent_Injuries/Coaches_Resources.aspx

Notes

INTRODUCTION

1. International Council for Coaching Excellence, Association of Summer Olympic International Federations, and Leeds Metropolitan University, *International Sport Coaching Framework* (Champaign, IL: Human Kinetics, 2013), 20–21.

2. John Lyle and Chris Cushion, *Sport Coaching Concepts: A Framework for Coaching Practice*, 2nd ed. (New York: Routledge, 2017), 61.

3. Daniel Gould and Jenny Nalepa, "Coaching Club and Scholastic Sport," in *Coach Education Essentials*, ed. Kristen Dieffenbach and Melissa Thompson (Champaign, IL: Human Kinetics, 2020), 112.

4. Nicholas L. Holt, Bethan C. Kingsley, Lisa N. Tink, and Jay Scherer, "Benefits and Challenges Associated with Sport Participation by Children and Parents from Low-Income Families," *Psychology of Sport and Exercise* 12, no. 5 (September 2011): 491–92, doi:10.1016/j.psychsport.2011.05.007.

5. Camilla J. Knight, Travis E. Dorsch, Keith V. Osai, Kyle L. Haderlie, and Paul A. Sellars, "Influences on Parental Involvement in Youth Sport," *Sport, Exercise, and Performance Psychology* 5, no. 2 (2016): 173–74, doi:10.1037/spy0000053.

6. Gould and Nalepa, 112.

7. Matthew T. Bowers, Laurence Chalip, and B. Christine Green, "Youth Sport Development in the United States and the Illusion of Synergy," in *Routledge Handbook of Sports Development*, ed. Barrie Houlihan and Mick Green (New York: Routledge, 2011), 177.

8. Lori Gano-Overway, Melissa Thompson, and Pete Van Mullem, *National Standards for Sport Coaches: Quality Coaches, Quality Sports* (Burlington, MA: Jones & Bartlett Learning, 2020), 31.

9. Gano-Overway et al., 31.

10. Melissa Murray, Linda Schoenstedt, and Drew Zwald, "Recommended Requisites for Sport Coaches," *Journal of Physical Education, Recreation & Dance* 84, no. 8 (2013), doi:10.1080/07303084.2013.832968.

11. "Explore Coaching," SHAPE America, accessed July 21, 2020, https://www.shape america.org/events/explorecoaching.

12. "Coaching Youth Sports," NAYS Coach Training, National Alliance for Youth Sport, accessed March 12, 2020, https://www.nays.org/nyscaonline/preview/coach ing-youth-sports.cfm.

13. "New and Renewing Coaches," Coach Membership: Requirements Checklist, USA Swimming, accessed September 16, 2020, https://www.usaswimming.org/ utility/landing-pages/coach-membership-checklist.

14. "National Standards for Sport Coaching," SHAPE America, accessed September 16, 2020, https://www.shapeamerica.org/standards/coaching/.

15. United States Olympic and Paralympic Committee (USOPC), *Quality Coaching Framework* (Champaign, IL: Human Kinetics).

CHAPTER 1. TO COACH IS TO KNOW YOUR WHY

1. Daniel Gould, "Quality Coaching Counts," *Phi Delta Kappan* 97, no. 8 (2016): 13–14.

2. Garrett Beatty and Bradley Fawver, "What Is the Status of Youth Coach Training in the U.S.?," *Research Brief*, The Aspen Institute's Project Play (2013), University of Florida, Sport Policy and Research Collaborative: 1.

3. Nicholas Holt, *Positive Youth Development through Sport* (New York: Routledge, 2016).

4. Wade Gilbert and Pierre Trudel, "Role of the Coach: How Model Youth Team Sport Coaches Frame Their Roles," *The Sport Psychologist* 18, no. 1 (2004): 21–43, doi:10.1123/tsp.18.1.21.

5. Ross Lorimer and David Holland-Smith, "Why Coach? A Case Study of the Prominent Influences on a Top-Level UK Outdoor Adventure Coach," *The Sport Psychologist* 26, no. 4 (2012): 571–83, doi:10.1123/tsp.26.4.571.

6. Joe Ehrmann, with Paula Ehrmann and Gregory Jordan, *InSideOut Coaching: How Sports Can Transform Lives* (New York: Simon & Schuster, 2011), 109.

7. Ehrmann et al., 110.

8. Martin Camiré, Tanya Forneris, Pierre Trudel, and Dany Bernard, "Strategies for Helping Coaches Facilitate Positive Youth Development through Sport," *Journal of Sport Psychology in Action* 2, no. 2 (2011): 94, doi:10.1080/21520704.2011.584246.

9. Douglas Hochstetler, "Coaching Philosophy, Values, and Ethics," in *Coaching for Sports Performance*, ed. Tim Baghurst (New York: Routledge, 2020), 20.

CHAPTER 2. TO COACH IS TO KNOW YOUR ROLE

1. Mike Krzyzewski and Jamie Spatola, *The Gold Standard: Building a World Class Team* (New York: Business Plus, 2009), 4–10.

2. "Meet Coach K," *Coach K* (website), accessed July 20, 2020, https://coachk.com/meet-coach-k/.

3. Krzyzewski and Spatola, 75–77.

4. James M. Kouzes and Barry Posner, *The Leadership Challenge: How to Make Extraordinary Things Happen in Organizations*, 6th ed. (Hoboken, NJ: John Wiley & Sons, 2017), 47–51.

5. Jean Côté and Wade Gilbert, "An Integrative Definition of Coaching Effectiveness and Expertise," *International Journal of Sports Science & Coaching* 4, no. 3 (2009): 312–15, https://doi.org/10.1260/174795409789623892.

6. Robin S. Vealey, Melissa A. Chase, and Robin Cooley, "Developing Self-Confidence in Young Athletes," in *Sport Psychology for Young Athletes*, ed. Camilla J. Knight, Chris G. Harwood, and Daniel Gould (New York: Routledge, 2018), 94.

7. *"Coach Pat Summitt: 1952–2016*," accessed July 20, 2020, https://utsports.com/sports/2017/6/20/coach-pat-summitt-1952-2016.aspx.

8. Pat Summitt and Sally Jenkins, *Reach for the Summit: The Definite Dozen System for Succeeding at Whatever You Do* (New York: Broadway, 1998), 8.

9. Summitt and Jenkins, 7.

10. Summitt and Jenkins, 120.

11. Summitt and Jenkins, 121–24.

CHAPTER 3. TO COACH IS TO BE A ROLE MODEL

1. Thomas Lickona, *Educating for Character: How Our Schools Can Teach Respect and Responsibility* (New York: Bantam Books, 1991), 52–54.

2. Lickona, 53–56.

3. Lickona, 58–59.

4. Lickona, 62–63.

5. Sharon K. Stoll and Jennifer M. Beller, "Ethical Dilemmas in College Sport," in *New Game Plan for College Sport*, ed. Richard E. Lapchick (Santa Barbara, CA: Praeger, 2006), 85.

6. Richard Goldstein, "Joe Paterno, Longtime Penn State Coach, Dies at 85," *New York Times*, January 23, 2012, https://www.nytimes.com/2012/01/23/sports/ncaafootball/joe-paterno-longtime-penn-state-coach-dies-at-85.html.

7. Goldstein.

8. Freeh Sporkin & Sullivan, LLP, "The Freeh Report: Report of the Special Investigative Counsel Regarding the Actions of The Pennsylvania State University Related to the Child Sexual Abuse Committed by Gerald A. Sandusky, 2012, *New York Times* (archives), accessed July 30, 2020, https://archive.nytimes.com/www.nytimes.com/interactive/2012/07/12/sports/ncaafootball/13pennstate-document.html?ref=ncaafootball.

9. Mark Memmott, "Penn State Coach Paterno to Retire, Says 'I Wish I Had Done More,'" *National Public Radio*, November 9, 2011, https://www.npr.org/sections/thetwo-way/2011/11/09/142171189/son-says-penn-state-coach-paterno-will-retire-at-end-of-season.

10. Angela Lumpkin, Sharon Kay Stoll, and Jennifer M. Beller, *Sport Ethics: Applications for Fair Play* (New York: McGraw-Hill, 2002), 21.

11. David L. Shields and Brenda L. Bredemeier, "Sport and the Development of Character" in *Handbook of Moral and Character Education*, ed. Larry P. Nucci and Darcia Narvaez (New York: Routledge, 2008), 512.

12. Albert Bandura, "Social Cognitive Theory of Moral Thought and Action," in *Handbook of Moral Behavior and Development*, ed. William M. Kurtines and Jacob L. Gewirtz (Mahwah, NJ: Lawrence Erlbaum Associates, 1991).

13. "Roger Federer Calls on Tennis Players to Respect Ballboys and Ballgirls," *Reuters*, October 9, 2018, https://www.theguardian.com/sport/2018/oct/09/roger-federer-calls-on-tennis-players-to-respect-ballboys-and-ballgirls.

CHAPTER 4. TO COACH IS TO BUILD RELATIONSHIPS

1. Dean Smith, Gerald D. Bell, and John Kilgo, *The Carolina Way: Leadership Lessons from a Life in Coaching* (New York: Penguin, 2004), 4.

2. Smith et al., 254.

3. Daniel J. A. Rhind and Sophia Jowett, "Relationship Maintenance Strategies in the Coach-Athlete Relationship: The Development of the COMPASS Model," *Journal of Applied Sport Psychology* 22, no. 1 (2010): 106–21, http://doi:10.1080/10413200903474472.

4. Sophia Jowett and Vaithehy Shanmugam, "Relational Coaching in Sport: Its Psychological Underpinnings and Practical Effectiveness," in *Routledge International Handbook of Sport Psychology*, ed. Robert Schinke, Kerry R. McGannon, and Brett Smith (London: Routledge, 2016).

5. Mary D. Fry and E. Whitney G. Moore, "Motivation in Sport: Theory and Application," in *APA Handbook of Sport and Exercise Psychology: Vol. 1. Sport Psychology*, ed. Mark H. Anshel (Washington, DC: American Psychological Association, 2019).

6. Jowett and Shanmugam, 471–84.

7. Rhind and Jowett, 106–21.

8. Mary D. Fry, Lori A. Gano-Overway, Marta Guivernau, Mi-Sook Kim, and Maria Newton, *A Coach's Guide to Maximizing the Youth Sport Experience: Work Hard, Be Kind* (London: Routledge, 2020).

9. Cameron Klein, Renée E. DeRouin, and Eduardo Salas, "Uncovering Workplace Interpersonal Skills: A Review, Framework, and Research Agenda," in *International Review of Industrial and Organizational Psychology*, Vol. 21, ed. Gerald P. Hodgkinson Leeds and J. Kevin Ford (Chichester, West Sussex, UK: John Wiley & Sons, 2006).

10. Klein et al., 79–126.

11. Robin S. Vealey, *Coaching for the Inner Edge* (Champaign, IL: Human Kinetics, 2005).

12. Vealey.

13. Daniel Goleman, "Leadership That Gets Results," *Harvard Business Review*. March–April 2000, 78–90.

184

CHAPTER 5. TO COACH IS TO SET THE CLIMATE

1. Gary Smith, "Running for Their Lives: The Story That Inspired *McFarland, USA*," *Sports Illustrated*, February 16, 2015: para 19, accessed August 25, 2020, https://www.si.com/high-school/2015/02/16/si-vault-running-their-lives-mcfarland-usa-movie-gary-smith.

2. Smith, para 16.

3. *Sport for Life, Sport for All: A Playbook to Get Every Kid in the Game* (Washington, DC: Aspen Institute, Project Play, 2015), 13.

4. Amanda J. Visek, Sara M. Achrati, Heather Manning, Karen McDonnell, Brandonn S. Harris, and Loretta DiPietro, "The Fun Integration Theory: Towards Sustaining Children and Adolescents Sport Participation," *Journal of Physical Activity & Health* 12, no. 3 (2015): 424–33, https://doi:10.1123/jpah.2013-0180.

5. Mary D. Fry, Lori A. Gano-Overway, Marta Guivernau, Mi-Sook Kim, and Maria Newton, *A Coach's Guide to Maximizing the Youth Sport Experience: Work Hard, Be Kind* (London: Routledge, 2020).

6. Susan Halden-Brown, *Mistakes Worth Making: How to Turn Sports Errors into Athletic Excellence* (Champaign, IL: Human Kinetics, 2003).

7. Halden-Brown, 123–27.

8. Shawn Ladda, "Creating Respectful and Inclusive Environments: The Role of Physical Educators and Coaches," *Journal of Physical Education, Recreation & Dance* 87, no. 3 (2016): 3–4, https://doi.org/10.1080/07303084.2016.1131536.

9. Pete Van Mullem and Don Showalter, "End on a Positive," *PHE America* (Physical & Health Education America Website), October 9, 2019: para 4, accessed August 25, 2020, https://www.pheamerica.org/2019/end-on-a-positive-3-minute-read/.

10. Joan L. Duda, Paul R. Appleton, Juliette Stebbings, and Isabel Balaguer, "Towards More Empowering and Less Disempowering Environments in Youth Sport: Theory to Evidence-Based Practice," in *Sport Psychology for Young Athletes*, ed. Camilla J. Knight, Chris G. Harwood, and Daniel Gould (New York: Routledge, 2018).

11. Geneviève A. Mageau and Robert J. Vallerand, "The Coach–Athlete Relationship: A Motivational Model," *Journal of Sports Science* 21, no. 11 (2003): 883–904, https://doi.org/10.1080/0264041031000140374.

CHAPTER 6. TO COACH IS TO KEEP ATHLETES SAFE

1. Marissa Frangione, Christina Mayfield, Andy Walsh, Kimberlee Bethany, and Nick Galli, "Hazing in Sport," *SportPsych Works* 5, no. 2 (2017), https://www.apa divisions.org/division-47/publications/sportpsych-works/hazing-sport.pdf.

2. "Bystander Revolution," accessed July 27, 2020, https://www.bystander revolution.org/.

3. William Oates and Casey Barlow, "An Injury Prevention Curriculum for Coaches," *Stop Sport Injuries*," (2011), https://www.stopsportsinjuries.org/STOP/ Downloads/Resources/CoachesCurriculumToolkit.pdf.

4. Ben Desbrow, Joanna McCormack, Louise M. Burke, Gregory R. Cox, Kieran Fallon, Matthew Hislop, Ruth Logan et al.,"Sports Dietitians Australia Position Statement: Sports Nutrition for the Adolescent Athlete," *International Journal of Sport Nutrition and Exercise Metabolism* 24, no. 5 (2014): 570–84, https://doi.org/ 10.1123/ijsnem.2014-0031.

5. Brendon P. McDermott, Scott A. Anderson, Lawrence E. Armstrong, Douglas J. Casa, Samuel N. Cheuvront, Larry Cooper, W. Larry Kenney, Francis G. O'Connor, and William O. Roberts, "National Athletic Trainers' Association Position Statement: Fluid Replacement for the Physically Active," *Journal of Athletic Training* 52, no. 9 (2017): 877–95, https://doi.org/10.4085/1062-6050-52.9.02.

6. Jennifer Sacheck and Nicole Schultz, "Optimal Nutrition for Youth Athletes: Food Sources and Fuel Timing," *National Youth Sports Health & Safety Institute*, (2016), http://nyshsi.org/wp-content/uploads/2012/08/NYSHSI-Optimal-Nutrition -for-Youth-Athletes.pdf.

7. Carolyn C. Jimenez, Matthew H. Corcoran, James T. Crawley, W. Guyton Hornsby Jr., Kimberly S. Peer, Rick D. Philbin, and Michael C. Riddell, "National Athletic Trainers' Association Position Statement: Management of the Athlete with Type 1 Diabetes Mellitus," *Journal of Athletic Training* 42, no. 4 (2007): 536–45.

8. Desbrow et al., 570–84.

9. Jimenez et al., 536.

10. "Eastern New York U10 Practice Plans by Week," accessed July 27, 2020, http:// www.enysoccer.com/coach_central/u10_practice_plans_by_week/.

11. Heather Mangieri, "Healthy Hydration for Young Athletes," *NATA News*, (July 2018): 18–20, https://www.nata.org/sites/default/files/healthy-hydration-for-young-athletes.pdf.

CHAPTER 7. TO COACH IS TO PLAN

1. John Wooden and Steve Jamison, *Wooden on Leadership* (New York: McGraw-Hill, 2005), 154.

2. Istvan Bayli, Richard Way, and Colin Higgs, *Long-Term Athlete Development* (Champaign, IL: Human Kinetics, 2013).

3. Colin Higgs, Richard Way, Vicki Harber, Paula Jurbala, and Istvan Bayli, *Long-Term Development in Sport and Physical Activity 3.0* (Canada: Sport for Life Society, 2019).

4. Bayli et al.

5. Higgs et al., 20–37.

6. "International Physical Literacy Association," accessed August 25, 2020, https://www.physical-literacy.org.uk/.

7. Higgs et al.

8. Bayli et al.

9. Don Hellison, *Teaching Personal and Social Responsibility through Physical Activity*, 3rd ed. (Champaign, IL: Human Kinetics, 2011).

10. Bayli et al., 83.

11. Rhodri Lloyd and Jon Oliver, "The Youth Physical Development Model: A New Approach to Long-Term Athletic Development," *Strength and Conditioning Journal*, 34, no. 3 (2012): 61–72, doi:10.1519/SSC.0b013e31825760ea.

12. Bayli et al., 81–91.

13. *Journal of Athletic Training* Releases Special Thematic Issue Focused on Youth Sports Specialization," *National Athletic Trainers' Association* (website), October 21, 2019, https://www.nata.org/press-release/102119/journal-athletic-training-releases-special-thematic-issue-focused-youth-sport.

14. "American Development Model," United States Olympic and Paralympic Committee, accessed September 20, 2020, https://www.teamusa.org/About-the-USOPC/Coaching-Education/American-Development-Model.

15. Higgs et al., 25.

16. "American Development Model."

17. "American Development Exit Competencies," USA Swimming, accessed September 10, 2020, https://www.usaswimming.org/coaches/popular-resources/american-development-model.

18. Rainer Martens, *Successful Coaching*, 4th ed. (Champaign, IL: Human Kinetics, 2012), 228–31.

19. Martens, 236.

20. Gregory Haff and Kristina Kendall, "Strength and Conditioning," in *Coaching for Sports Performance*, ed. Timothy Baghurst (New York: Routledge, 2020): 310.

21. Haff et al., 311.

22. Haff and Kendall, 313.

23. Haff and Kendall, 331.

24. Martens, 241.

25. Amy Price, Dave Collins, John Stoszkowski, and Shane Pill, "Strategic Understandings: An Investigation of Professional Academy Youth Soccer Coaches' Interpretation, Knowledge, and Application of Game Strategies," *International Sport Coaching Journal* 7, no. 2 (2020): 1–12.

26. Damon Burton and Thomas D. Raedeke, *Sport Psychology for Coaches* (Champaign, IL: Human Kinetics, 2008), 36–42.

27. Robin S. Vealey, "Mental Skills Training in Sport," in *Handbook of Sport Psychology*, ed. Gershon Tenenbaum and Robert C. Eklund (Hoboken, NJ: John Wiley & Sons, 2007), 288–91.

28. Steve J. Danish and Valerie C. Nellen, "New Roles for Sport Psychologists: Teaching Life Skills through Sport to At-Risk Youth," *Quest* 49, no. 1 (1997): 102, https://doi.org/10.1080/00336297.1997.10484226.

29. Lorcan D. Cronin and Justine Allen, "Development and Initial Validation of the Life Skills Scale for Sport," *Psychology of Sport and Exercise* 28 (2017), 105–19, https://doi.org/10.1016/j.psychsport.2016.11.001.

30. Martin Camiré, Tanya Forneris, Pierre Trudel, and Dany Bernard, "Strategies for Helping Coaches Facilitate Positive Youth Development through Sport,"

Journal of Sport Psychology in Action 2, no. 2 (2011): 92, https://doi.org/10.1080/2 1520704.2011.584246.

31. Camiré et al., 92–99.

32. Kelsey Kendellen, Martin Camiré, Corliss N. Bean, Tanya Forneris, and Jeff Thompson, "Integrating Life Skills into Golf Canada's Youth Programs: Insights into a Successful Research to Practice Partnership," *Journal of Sport Psychology in Action* 8, no. 1 (2017): 34–46, https://doi.org/10.1080/21520704.2016.1205699.

CHAPTER 8. TO COACH IS TO TEACH

1. Melissa Jensen, "Pedagogy of Coaching," in *Coaching for Sports Performance*, ed. Timothy Baghurst (New York: Routledge, 2020), 50.

2. Jensen, 50–51.

3. Paul Kinnerk, Stephen Harvey, Ciarán MacDonncha, and Mark Lyons, "A Review of the Game-Based Approaches to Coaching Literature in Competitive Team Sport Settings," *Quest* 70, no. 4 (2018): 401.

4. Alan Launder and Wendy Piltz, *Play Practice: Engaging and Developing Skilled Players from Beginner to Elite* (Champaign, IL: Human Kinetics, 2013).

5. Launder and Piltz, 39–53.

6. Albert Bandura, *Social Learning Theory* (Englewood Cliffs, NJ: Prentice Hall, 1976).

7. Bandura.

8. Cheryl A. Coker, *Motor Learning and Control for Practitioners*, 4th ed. (New York: Routledge, 2018), 235–43.

9. Rainer Martens, *Successful Coaching*, 4th ed. (Champaign, IL: Human Kinetics, 2012), 228–81.

10. Amy Price, Dave Collins, John Stoszkowski, and Shane Pill, "Strategic Understandings: An Investigation of Professional Academy Youth Soccer Coaches' Interpretation, Knowledge, and Application of Game Strategies," *International Sport Coaching Journal* 7, no. 2 (2020): 151–62.

11. Stephen A. Mitchell, Judith L. Oslin, and Linda L. Griffin, *Teaching Sport Concepts and Skills* (Champaign, IL: Human Kinetics, 2006), 7–10.

12. David Cooper and Barrie Gordon, eds., *Tactical Decision-Making in Sport: How Coaches Can Help Athletes to Make Better In-Game Decisions* (New York: Routledge, 2020).

13. Coker, 313–16.

14. Thelma Horn, "Examining the Impact of Coaches' Feedback Patterns on the Psychosocial Well-Being of Youth Sport Athletes," *Kinesiology Review* 8, no. 3 (2019): 244–51, https://doi.org/10.1123/kr.2019-0017.

15. Coker, 312–13.

16. Tony Dicicco, Colleen Hacker, and Charles Salzberg, *Catch Them Being Good: Everything You Need to Know to Successfully Coach Girls* (New York: Penguin, 2003).

17. Horn, 246–47.

18. Coker, 312.

CHAPTER 9. TO COACH IS TO ASSESS

1. *Core Skills*, Long Term Field Hockey Development, Resource Centre, Field Hockey, Canada, accessed August 27, 2020, http://lthd.fieldhockey.ca/en/page-20--core-6-skills

2. Jamie Collins and Natalie Durand-Bush, "Strategies Used by an Elite Curling Coach to Nurture Athletes' Self-Regulation: A Single Case Study," *Journal of Applied Sport Psychology* 26, no. 2 (2014): 211–13, doi:10.1080/10413200.2013.819823.

3. Pia Nilsson, Lynn Marriott, and Ron Sirak, *Every Shot Must Have a Purpose* (New York: Penguin, 2005).

CHAPTER 10. TO COACH IS TO ADAPT

1. Dictionary.com, s.v. "adapt," accessed August 27, 2020, https://www.dictionary.com/browse/adapt.

2. Leon Megginson, "Lessons from Europe for American Business," *Southwestern Social Science Quarterly* 44, no. 1 (1963): 4.

3. Tasha Eurich, "What Self-Awareness Really Is (and How to Cultivate It)," *Harvard Business Review*, January 4, 2018, accessed September 5, 2020, https://hbr.org/2018/01/what-self-awareness-really-is-and-how-to-cultivate-it.

4. Eurich.

5. Eurich.

6. Zoe Knowles, David Gilbourne, Andy Borrie, and Alan Nevill, "Developing the Reflective Sports Coach: A Study Exploring the Processes of Reflective Practice

within a Higher Education Coaching Programme," *Reflective Practice* 2, no. 2 (2001): 185–207.

7. John Lyle and Chris Cushion, *Sport Coaching Concepts: A Framework for Coaching Practice*, 2nd ed. (New York: Routledge, 2017), 170.

CHAPTER 11. TO COACH IS TO GET BETTER EVERY DAY

1. Jean Côté and Wade Gilbert, "An Integrative Definition of Coaching Effectiveness and Expertise, *International Journal of Sports Science & Coaching* 4, no. 3 (2009): 307–23.

2. Côté and Gilbert.

3. Lee J. Nelson, Christopher J. Cushion, and Paul Potrac, "Formal, Nonformal, and Informal Coach Learning: A Holistic Conceptualisation," *International Journal of Sports Science & Coaching* 1, no. 3 (2006): 247–59, https://doi.org/10.1260/174795406778604627.

4. Donald Schön, *Educating the Reflective Practitioner* (San Francisco: Jossey-Bass, 1987).

5. Jennifer A. Moon, *A Handbook of Reflective and Experiential Learning: Theory and Practice* (New York: Routledge, 2013).

6. Zoe Knowles, David Gilbourne, Andy Borrie, and Alan Nevill, "Developing the Reflective Sports Coach: A Study Exploring the Processes of Reflective Practice within a Higher Education Coaching Programme," *Reflective Practice* 2, no. 2 (2001): 185–207.

7. Wade Gilbert and Pierre Trudel, "Learning to Coach through Experience: Reflection in Model Youth Sport Coaches," *Journal of Teaching in Physical Education* 21, no. 1 (2001): 16–34, https://doi.org/10.1123/jtpe.21.1.16.

8. Andy Gillham and Pete Van Mullem, "Coaching the Coach: Helping Coaches Improve Their Performance," in *Coaching for Human Development and Performance in Sports*, ed. Rui Resende and A. Rui Gomes (Lausanne: Springer International Publishing [in press]).

9. D. Randy Garrison, "Self-Directed Learning: Toward a Comprehensive Model," *Adult Education Quarterly* 48, no. 1 (1997): 18–33, https://doi.org/10.1177/074171369704800103.

10. John Lyle and Chris Cushion, *Sports Coaching Concepts: A Framework for Coaching Practice* (London: Routledge, 2017), 103–204.

11. Pete Van Mullem and Chris Croft, "Planning Your Journey in Coaching: Building a Network for Long-Term Success," *Strategies: A Journal for Physical and Sport Educators* 28, no. 6 (2015): 15–22, https://doi.org/10.1080/08924562.2015.1087903.

12. Gillham and Van Mullem.

13. Pete Van Mullem, "Snow Valley: A Learning Environment for Coaches," *PHE America* (March 6, 2020), https://www.pheamerica.org/2020/snow-valley-a-learning-environment-for-coaches/.

14. Etienne Wenger, *Communities of Practice: Learning, Meaning, and Identity* (Cambridge, UK, Cambridge University Press, 1998).

Bibliography

"American Development Exit Competencies." USA Swimming. Accessed September 10, 2020. https://www.usaswimming.org/docs/default-source/coaching-resources documents/american-development-model-for-swimming.pdf.

"American Development Model." United States Olympic and Paralympic Committee. Accessed September 20, 2020. https://www.teamusa.org/About-the-USOPC/ Coaching-Education/American-Development-Model.

Bandura, Albert. *Social Learning Theory.* Englewood Cliffs, NJ: Prentice Hall, 1976.

Bandura, Albert. "Social Cognitive Theory of Moral Thought and Action." In *Handbook of Moral Behavior and Development*, edited by William M. Kurtines and Jacob L. Gewirtz, pp. 45–103. Mahwah, NJ: Lawrence Erlbaum Associates, 1991.

Bayli, Istvan, Richard Way, and Colin Higgs. *Long-Term Athlete Development.* Champaign, IL: Human Kinetics, 2013.

Beatty, Garrett, and Bradley Fawver. "What Is the Status of Youth Coach Training in the U.S.?" *Research Brief*, The Aspen Institute's Project Play. University of Florida, *Sport Policy and Research Collaborative*, 2013.

Bowers, Matthew T., Laurence Chalip, and B. Christine Green. "Youth Sport Development in the United States and the Illusion of Synergy." In *Routledge Handbook of Sports Development*, edited by Barrie Houlihan and Mick Green, pp. 173–83. New York: Routledge, 2011.

Burton, Damon and Thomas D. Raedeke. *Sport Psychology for Coaches*. Champaign, IL: Human Kinetics, 2008.

"Bystander Revolution." Accessed July 27, 2020. https://www.bystanderrevolution.org/.

Camiré, Martin, Tanya Forneris, Pierre Trudel, and Dany Bernard. "Strategies for Helping Coaches Facilitate Positive Youth Development through Sport." *Journal of Sport Psychology in Action* 2, no. 2 (2011): 92–99. https://doi.org/10.1080/21520 704.2011.584246.

"Coaching Youth Sports." NAYS Coach Training, National Alliance for Youth Sport. Accessed March 12, 2020. https://www.nays.org/nyscaonline/preview/coaching-youth-sports.cfm.

"*Coach Pat Summitt: 1952–2016*." Accessed July 20, 2020. https://utsports.com/sports/2017/6/20/coach-pat-summitt-1952-2016.aspx.

Coker, Cheryl A. *Motor Learning and Control for Practitioners*, 4th ed. New York: Routledge, 2018.

Collins, Jamie and Natalie Durand-Bush. "Strategies Used by an Elite Curling Coach to Nurture Athletes' Self-Regulation: A Single Case Study." *Journal of Applied Sport Psychology* 26, no. 2 (2014): 211–24. https://doi.org/10.1080/10413200.201.819823.

Cooper, David and Barrie Gordon. *Tactical Decision-Making in Sport: How Coaches Can Help Athletes to Make Better In-Game Decisions*. New York: Routledge, 2020.

Core Skills. Long Term Field Hockey Development, Resource Centre Field Hockey Canada. Accessed August 27, 2020. http://lthd.fieldhockey.ca/en/page-20--core -6-skills.

Côté, Jean and Wade Gilbert. "An Integrative Definition of Coaching Effectiveness and Expertise." *International Journal of Sports Science & Coaching* 4, no. 3 (2009): 307–23. https://doi.org/10.1260/174795409789623892.

Cronin, Lorcan D. and Justine Allen. "Development and Initial Validation of the Life Skills Scale for Sport." *Psychology of Sport and Exercise* 28 (2017): 105–19.

Crow, R. Brian and Eric W. Macintosh. "Conceptualizing a Meaningful Definition of Hazing in Sport." *European Sport Management Quarterly* 9, no. 4 (2009): 433–51. https://doi.org/10.1080/16184740903331937.

Danish, Steve J. and Valerie C. Nellen. "New Roles for Sport Psychologists: Teaching: Life Skills through Sport to At-Risk Youth." *Quest* 49, no. 1 (1997): 100–13. https://doi.org/10.1080/00336297.1997.10484226.

Desbrow, Ben, Joanna McCormack, Louise M. Burke, Gregory R. Cox, Kieran Fallon, Matthew Hislop, Ruth Logan et al. "Sports Dietitians Australia Position Statement: Sports Nutrition for the Adolescent Athlete." *International Journal of Sport Nutrition and Exercise Metabolism* 24, no. 5 (2014): 570–84. https://doi .org/10.1123/ijsnem.2014-0031.

Dicicco, Tony, Colleen Hacker, and Charles Salzberg. *Catch Them Being Good: Everything You Need to Know to Successfully Coach Girls.* New York: Penguin, 2003.

Duda, Joan L., Paul R. Appleton, Juliette Stebbings, and Isabel Balaguer. "Towards More Empowering and Less Disempowering Environments in Youth Sport: Theory to Evidence-Based Practice." In *Sport Psychology for Young Athletes*, edited by Camilla J. Knight, Chris G. Harwood, and Daniel Gould, pp. 81–93. New York: Routledge, 2018.

"Eastern New York U10 Practice Plans by Week." Accessed July 27, 2020. http:// www.enysoccer.com/coach_central/u10_practice_plans_by_week/.

Ehrmann, Joe, with Paula Ehrmann and Gregory Jordan. *InSideOut Coaching: How Sports Can Transform Lives.* New York: Simon & Schuster, 2011.

Eurich, Tasha. "What Self-Awareness Really Is (and How to Cultivate It)." *Harvard Business Review*, January 4, 2018. https://hbr.org/2018/01/what-self-awareness -really-is-and-how-to-cultivate-it.

"Explore Coaching." SHAPE America. Accessed July 21, 2020. https://www.shape america.org/events/explorecoaching.

Frangione, Marissa, Christina Mayfield, Andy Walsh, Kimberlee Bethany, and Nick Galli. "Hazing in Sport." *SportPsych Works* 5, no. 2 (2017). Accessed July 27, 2020. https://www.apadivisions.org/division-47/publications/sportpsych-works/ hazing-sport.pdf.

Freeh Sporkin & Sullivan, LLP. "The Freeh Report: Report of the Special Investigative Counsel Regarding the Actions of The Pennsylvania State University Related to the Child Sexual Abuse Committed by Gerald A. Sandusy." 2012. *New York Times* (archives). https://archive.nytimes.com/www.nytimes .com/interactive/2012/07/12/sports/ncaafootball/13pennstate-document.html ?ref=ncaafootball.

Fry, Mary D., Lori A. Gano-Overway, Marta Guivernau, Mi-Sook Kim, and Maria Newton. *A Coach's Guide to Maximizing the Youth Sport Experience: Work Hard, Be Kind.* London: Routledge, 2020.

Fry, Mary D. and E. Whitney G. Moore. "Motivation in Sport: Theory and Application." In *APA Handbook of Sport and Exercise Psychology: Vol. 1. Sport Psychology*, edited by Mark H. Anshel, pp. 273–99. Washington, DC: American Psychological Association, 2019.

Gano-Overway, Lori, Melissa Thompson, and Pete Van Mullem. *National Standards for Sport Coaches: Quality Coaches, Quality Sports*, 3rd ed. Burlington, MA: Jones & Bartlett Learning, 2020.

Garrison, D. Randy. "Self-Directed Learning: Toward a Comprehensive Model." *Adult Education Quarterly* 48, no. 1 (1997): 18–33. https://doi.org/10.1177/074171369704800103.

Gearity, Brian T. "Autoethnography." In *Research Methods in Sport Coaching*, edited by Lee Nelson, Ryan Groom, and Paul Potrac, pp. 205–16. New York: Routledge, 2014.

Gilbert, Wade and Pierre Trudel. "Learning to Coach through Experience: Reflection in Model Youth Sport Coaches." *Journal of Teaching in Physical Education* 21, no. 1 (2001): 16–34. https://doi.org/10.1123/jtpe.21.1.16.

Gilbert, Wade and Pierre Trudel. "Role of the Coach: How Model Youth Team Sport Coaches Frame Their Roles." *The Sport Psychologist* 18, no. 1 (2004): 21–43. https://doi.org/10.1123/tsp.18.1.21.

Gillham, Andy and Pete Van Mullem. "Coaching the Coach: Helping Coaches Improve Their Performance." In *Coaching for Human Development and Performance in Sports*, edited by Rui Resende and A. Rui Gomes. Lausanne: Springer International Publishing, 2021.

Goldstein, Richard. "Joe Paterno, Longtime Penn State Coach, Dies at 85." *New York Times*, January 23, 2012. https://www.nytimes.com/2012/01/23/sports/ncaafootball/joe-paterno-longtime-penn-state-coach-dies-at-85.html.

Goleman, Daniel. "Leadership That Gets Results." *Harvard Business Review*, March–April 2000, 78–90.

Gould, Daniel. "Quality Coaching Counts." *Phi Delta Kappan* 97, no. 8 (2016): 13–18.

Gould, Daniel and Jenny Nalepa. "Coaching Club and Scholastic Sport." In *Coach Education Essentials*, edited by Kristen Dieffenbach and Melissa Thompson, pp. 111–30. Champaign, IL: Human Kinetics, 2020.

Haff, Gregory and Kristina Kendall. "Strength and Conditioning." In *Coaching for Sports Performance*, edited by Timothy Baghurst, pp. 309–50. New York: Routledge, 2020.

Halden-Brown, Susan. *Mistakes Worth Making: How to Turn Sports Errors into Athletic Excellence*. Champaign, IL: Human Kinetics, 2003.

"Harassment." U.S. Equal Employment Opportunity Commission. Accessed September 21, 2020. https://www.eeoc.gov/harassment.

Hellison, Don. *Teaching Personal and Social Responsibility through Physical Activity*, 3rd ed. Champaign, IL: Human Kinetics, 2011.

Higgs, Colin, Richard Way, Vicki Harber, Paula Jurbala, and Istvan Bayli. *Long-Term Development in Sport and Physical Activity 3.0*. Canada: Sport for Life Society, 2019.

Hochstetler, Douglas. "Coaching Philosophy, Values, and Ethics." In *Coaching for Sports Performance*, edited by Tim Baghurst, pp. 11–38. New York: Routledge, 2020.

Holt, Nicholas. *Positive Youth Development through Sport*. New York: Routledge, 2016.

Holt, Nicholas L., Bethan C. Kingsley, Lisa N. Tink, and Jay Scherer. "Benefits and Challenges Associated with Sport Participation by Children and Parents from Low-Income Families." *Psychology of Sport and Exercise* 12, no. 5 (2011): 490–99. https://doi.org/10.1016/j.psychsport.2011.05.007.

Horn, Thelma. "Examining the Impact of Coaches' Feedback Patterns on the Psychosocial Well-Being of Youth Sport Athletes." *Kinesiology Review* 8, no. 3 (2019): 244–51. https://doi.org/10.1123/kr.2019-0017.

Hughes, Ceri, Sarah Lee, and Gavin Chesterfield. "Innovation in Sports Coaching: The Implementation of Reflective Cards." *Reflective Practice* 10, no. 3 (2009): 367–84. https://doi.org/10.1080/14623940903034895.

International Council for Coaching Excellence (ICCE), Association of Summer Olympic International Federations (ASOIF), and Leeds Metropolitan University. *International Sport Coaching Framework*. Champaign, IL: Human Kinetics, 2013.

"International Physical Literacy Association." Accessed August 25, 2020. https://www.physical-literacy.org.uk/.

Jensen, Melissa. "Pedagogy of Coaching." In *Coaching for Sports Performance*, edited by Timothy Baghurst, pp. 38–75. New York: Routledge, 2020.

Jimenez, Carolyn C., Matthew H. Corcoran, James T. Crawley, W. Guyton Hornsby Jr., Kimberly S. Peer, Rick D. Philbin, and Michael C. Riddell. "National Athletic Trainers' Association Position Statement: Management of the Athlete with Type 1 Diabetes Mellitus." *Journal of Athletic Training* 42, no. 4 (2007): 536–45.

"*Journal of Athletic Training* Releases Special Thematic Issue Focused on Youth Sports Specialization." *National Athletic Trainers' Association* (website), October 21, 2019. https://www.nata.org/press-release/102119/journal-athletic-training-releases-special-thematic-issue-focused-youth-sport.

Jowett, Sophia and Vaithehy Shanmugam. "Relational Coaching in Sport: Its Psychological Underpinnings and Practical Effectiveness." In *Routledge International Handbook of Sport Psychology*, edited by Robert Schinke, Kerry R. McGannon, and Brett Smith, pp. 471–84. London: Routledge, 2016.

Kasper, Korey. "Sports Training Principles." *Current Sports Medicine Reports* 18, no. 4 (2019): 95–99. https://journals.lww.com/acsm-csmr/fulltext/2019/04000/sports_training_principles.2.aspx.

Kendellen, Kelsey, Martin Camiré, Corliss N. Bean, Tanya Forneris, and Jeff Thompson. "Integrating Life Skills into Golf Canada's Youth Programs: Insights into a Successful Research to Practice Partnership." *Journal of Sport Psychology in Action* 8, no. 1 (2017): 34–46. https://doi.org/10.1080/21520704.2016.1205699.

Kinnerk, Paul, Stephen Harvey, Ciarán MacDonncha, and Mark Lyons. "A Review of the Game-Based Approaches to Coaching Literature in Competitive Team Sport Settings." *Quest* 70, no. 4 (2018): 401–18. https://doi.org/10.1080/00336297.2018.1439390.

Klein, Cameron, Renée E. DeRouin, and Eduardo Salas. "Uncovering Workplace Interpersonal Skills: A Review, Framework, and Research Agenda." In *International Review of Industrial and Organizational Psychology*, Vol. 21, edited by Gerald P. Hodgkinson Leeds and J. Kevin Ford, pp. 79–126. Chichester, West Sussex, UK: John Wiley & Sons, 2006.

Knight, Camilla J., Travis E. Dorsch, Keith V. Osai, Kyle L. Haderlie, and Paul A. Sellars. "Influences on Parental Involvement in Youth Sport." *Sport, Exercise, and Performance Psychology* 5, no. 2 (2016): 161–78. https://doi.org/10.1037/spy0000053.

Knowles, Zoe, David Gilbourne, Andy Borrie, and Alan Nevill. "Developing the Reflective Sports Coach: A Study Exploring the Processes of Reflective Practice within a Higher Education Coaching Programme." *Reflective Practice* 2, no. 2 (2001): 185–207. https://doi.org/10.1080/14623940123820.

Kouzes, James and Barry Posner. *The Leadership Challenge: How to Make Extraordinary Things Happen in Organizations*, 6th ed. Hoboken, NJ: John Wiley & Sons, 2017.

Krzyzewski, Mike and Jamie Spatola. *The Gold Standard: Building a World-Class Team*. New York: Business Plus, 2009.

Kuklick, Clayton R. and Michael Kasales. "Reflective Practice to Enhance Coach Development and Practice." In *Coach Education and Development in Sport: Instructional Strategies*, edited by Bettina Callary and Brian Gearity, pp. 76–77. New York: Routledge, 2019.

Ladda, Shawn. "Creating Respectful and Inclusive Environments: The Role of Physical Educators and Coaches." *Journal of Physical Education, Recreation & Dance* 87, no. 3 (2016): 3–4. https://doi.org/10.1080/07303084.2016.1131536.

Launder, Alan and Wendy Piltz. *Play Practice: Engaging and Developing Skilled Players from Beginner to Elite*. Champaign, IL: Human Kinetics, 2013.

Lickona, Thomas. *Educating for Character: How Our Schools Can Teach Respect and Responsibility*. New York: Bantam Books, 1991.

Lloyd, Rhodri and Jon Oliver. "The Youth Physical Development Model: A New Approach to Long-Term Athletic Development." *Strength and Conditioning Journal* 34, no. 3 (2012): 61–72. https://doi.org/10.1519/SSC.0b013e31825760ea.

Lorimer, Ross and David Holland-Smith. "Why Coach? A Case Study of the Prominent Influences on a Top-Level UK Outdoor Adventure Coach." *The Sport Psychologist* 26, no. 4 (2012): 571–83. https://doi.org/10.1123/tsp.26.4.571.

Lumpkin, Angela, Sharon Kay Stoll, and Jennifer M. Beller. *Sport Ethics: Applications for Fair Play*, 3rd ed. New York: McGraw-Hill, 2002.

Lyle, John and Chris Cushion. *Sport Coaching Concepts: A Framework for Coaching Practice*, 2nd ed. New York: Routledge, 2017.

Mageau, Geneviève A. and Robert J. Vallerand. "The Coach–Athlete Relationship: A Motivational Model." *Journal of Sports Science* 21, no. 11 (2003): 883–904. https://doi.org/10.1080/0264041031000140374.

Mangieri, Heather. "Healthy Hydration for Young Athletes: Ways to Prevent Fluid Loss from Becoming Detrimental." *NATA News*, July 2018, 18–20. https://www.nata.org/sites/default/files/healthy-hydration-for-young-athletes.pdf.

Martens, Rainer. *Successful Coaching*, 4th ed. Champaign, IL: Human Kinetics, 2012.

McDermott, Brendon P., Scott A. Anderson, Lawrence E. Armstrong, Douglas J. Casa, Samuel N. Cheuvront, Larry Cooper, W. Larry Kenney, Francis G. O'Connor, and William O. Roberts. "National Athletic Trainers' Association Position Statement: Fluid Replacement for the Physically Active." *Journal of Athletic Training* 52, no. 9 (2017): 877–95. https://doi.org/10.4085/1062-6050-52.9.02.

"Meet Coach K." *Coach K* (website). Accessed July 20, 2020. https://coachk.com/meet-coach-k/.

Megginson, Leon C. (1963). "Lessons from Europe for American Business." *Southwestern Social Science Quarterly* 44, no. 1 (1963): 3–13.

Memmott, Mark. "Penn State Coach Paterno to Retire, Says 'I Wish I Had Done More.'" *National Public Radio*, November 9, 2011. https://www.npr.org/sections/thetwo-way/2011/11/09/142171189/son-says-penn-state-coach-paterno-will-retire-at-end-of-season.

Mitchell, Stephen A., Judith L. Oslin, and Linda L. Griffin. *Teaching Sport Concepts and Skills*. Champaign, IL: Human Kinetics, 2006.

Moon, Jennifer A. *A Handbook of Reflective and Experiential Learning: Theory and Practice*. New York: Routledge, 2013.

Mosston, Muska and Sara Ashworth. *Teaching Physical Education: First Online Edition*. United States: Spectrum Institute for Teaching and Learning, 2008.

Murray, Melissa, Linda Schoenstedt, and Drew Zwald. "Recommended Requisites for Sport Coaches." *Journal of Physical Education, Recreation & Dance* 84, no. 8 (2013): 7–12. https://doi.org/10.1080/07303084.2013.832968.

"National Standards for Sport Coaching." SHAPE America. Accessed September 16, 2020. https://www.shapeamerica.org/standards/coaching/.

Nelson, Lee J., Christopher J. Cushion, and Paul Potrac. "Formal, Nonformal, and Informal Coach Learning: A Holistic Conceptualisation." *International Journal of Sports Science & Coaching* 1, no. 3 (2006): 247–59. https://doi.org/10.1260/174795406778604627.

"New and Renewing Coaches." Coach Membership: Requirements Checklist, USA Swimming. Accessed September 16, 2020. https://www.usaswimming.org/utility/landing-pages/coach-membership-checklist.

Nilsson, Pia, Lynn Marriott, and Ron Sirak. *Every Shot Must Have a Purpose*. New York: Penguin, 2005.

Oates, William and Casey Barlow. "An Injury Prevention Curriculum for Coaches: Stop Sport Injuries." 2011. https://www.stopsportsinjuries.org/STOP/Downloads/Resources/CoachesCurriculumToolkit.pdf.

Parent Toolkit. U.S. Center for Safe Sport. 2018.

Price, Amy, Dave Collins, John Stoszkowski, and Shane Pill. "Strategic Understandings: An Investigation of Professional Academy Youth Soccer Coaches' Interpretation, Knowledge, and Application of Game Strategies." *International Sport Coaching Journal* 7, no. 2 (2020): 1–12 (151–62).

Rhind, Daniel J. A. and Sophia Jowett. "Relationship Maintenance Strategies in the Coach-Athlete Relationship: The Development of the COMPASS Model." *Journal of Applied Sport Psychology* 22, no. 1 (2010): 106–21. http://doi:10.1080/10413200903474472.

"Roger Federer Calls on Tennis Players to Respect Ballboys and Ballgirls." *Reuters*, October 9, 2018. https://www.theguardian.com/sport/2018/oct/09/roger-federer-calls-on-tennis-players-to-respect-ballboys-and-ballgirls.

Sacheck, Jennifer and Nicole Schultz. "Optimal Nutrition for Youth Athletes: Food Sources and Fuel Timing." *National Youth Sports Health & Safety Institute*, 2016. http://nyshsi.org/wp-content/uploads/2012/08/NYSHSI-Optimal-Nutrition-for-Youth-Athletes.pdf.

Schön, Donald, *Educating the Reflective Practitioner*. San Francisco: Jossey-Bass, 1987.

Shields, David L. and Brenda L. Bredemeier. "Sport and the Development of Character." In *Handbook of Moral and Character Education*, edited by Larry P. Nucci and Darcia Narvaez, pp. 500–519. New York: Routledge, 2008.

Smith, Dean, Gerald D. Bell, and John Kilgo. *The Carolina Way: Leadership Lessons from a Life in Coaching*. New York: Penguin, 2004.

Smith, Gary. "Running for Their Lives: The Story That Inspired *McFarland, USA*." *Sports Illustrated*, February 16, 2015. https://www.si.com/high-school/2015/02/16/si-vault-running-their-lives-mcfarland-usa-movie-gary-smith.

Smith, Peter K.. "Bullying: Definition, Types, Causes, Consequences and Intervention." *Social and Personality Psychology Compass* 10, no. 9 (2016): 519–32. https://doi.org.10.1111/spc3.12266.

Sport for Life, Sport for All: A Playbook to Get Every Kid in the Game. Washington, DC: Aspen Institute, Project Play, 2015.

Stirling, Ashley E. and Gretchen A. Kerr. "Defining and Categorizing Emotional Abuse in Sport." *European Journal of Sport Science* 8, no. 4 (2008): 178. http://doi.org.10.1080/17461390802086281.

Stoll, Sharon K. and Jennifer M. Beller. "Ethical Dilemmas in College Sport." In *New Game Plan for College Sport*, edited by Richard E. Lapchick, pp. 75–91. Santa Barbara, CA: Praeger, 2006.

Summitt, Pat and Sally Jenkins. *Reach for the Summit: The Definite Dozen System for Succeeding at Whatever You Do.* New York: Broadway, 1998.

United States Olympic and Paralympic Committee (USOPC). *Quality Coaching Framework.* Champaign, IL: Human Kinetics, 2018.

Van Mullem, Pete. "Snow Valley: A Learning Environment for Coaches." *PHE America* (website), March 6, 2020. https://www.pheamerica.org/2020/snow-valley-a-learning-environment-for-coaches/.

Van Mullem, Pete and Chris Croft. "Planning Your Journey in Coaching: Building a Network for Long-Term Success." *Strategies: A Journal for Physical and Sport Educators* 28, no. 6 (2015): 15–22. https://doi.org/10.1080/08924562.2015.1087903.

Van Mullem, Pete and Don Showalter. "End on a Positive." *PHE America* (Physical & Health Education America website), October 9, 2019. https://www.pheamerica.org/2019/end-on-a-positive-3-minute-read/.

Vealey, Robin S. *Coaching for the Inner Edge.* Champaign, IL: Human Kinetics, 2005.

Vealey, Robin S. "Mental Skills Training in Sport." In *Handbook of Sport Psychology*, edited by Gershon Tenenbaum and Robert C. Eklund, pp. 288–91. Hoboken, NJ: John Wiley & Sons, 2007.

Vealey, Robin S., Melissa A. Chase, and Robin Cooley. "Developing Self-Confidence in Young Athletes." In *Sport Psychology for Young Athletes*, edited by Camilla J. Knight, Chris G. Harwood, and Daniel Gould, pp. 94–105. New York: Routledge, 2018.

Visek, Amanda, Sara M. Achrati, Heather Manning, Karen McDonnell, Brandonn S. Harris, and Loretta DiPietro. "The Fun Integration Theory: Towards Sustaining Children and Adolescents Sport Participation." *Journal of Physical Activity & Health* 12, no. 3 (2015): 424–33. https://doi:10.1123/jpah.2013-0180.

Wenger, Etienne. *Communities of Practice: Learning, Meaning, and Identity.* Cambridge, UK: Cambridge University Press, 1998.

Whitehead, Amy, Brendan Cropley, Tabo Huntley, Andy Miles, Laura Quayle, and Zoe Knowles. "'Think Aloud': Toward a Framework to Facilitate Reflective Practice amongst Rugby League Coaches." *International Sport Coaching Journal* 3, no. 3 (2016): 269–86. https://doi.org/10.1123/iscj.2016-0021.

Wooden, John and Steve Jamison. *Wooden on Leadership.* New York: McGraw-Hill, 2005.

Index

community of practice 170, 174–75
competence. *See* confidence
competitive strategy (strategies), 8, 31,
    97, 99, 109–10, 116, 119, 122, 132,
    164
conditioning. *See* physical conditioning
confidence, 24, 26–27, 32, 33, 99, 100,
    107, 111–14, *140*, 143, 145;
    competence, 26, *27*, 32, 34, 37, 99–
    100, 140, 170;
    developing confidence, 2, 16, 20, 31,
    70, 104–05;
    self-confidence, 59, 63, 156, 181n6
connection. *See* relationships
constructive feedback. *See* feedback
core values, 22–24;
    personal, 12, 19, 29–30, 40, 158, 173;
    organizational or team, 13, 22–25,
    28, 31–32, 60, 78, 84, 86, 141
culture. *See* climate

decision-making, 14, 53, 77, 79, 124–25,
    133, 154, 157–59;
    ethical decision making, 39–41,
    43–*44*, 49–50;
    games based, 125;
    tactical, 79, 132–33, 137, 188n12
demonstration. *See* instructional styles
discipline, 10, 29

emotional intelligence, 59, 62–64
empathy, 13–14, 26, 34, 37, 56, 75–75,
    82
ethical decision-making. *See* decision-
    making
ethical dilemma, 37–40, 43, 46, 48, 50
ethical mind set, 46, 48–50, 33–34, 36;
    moral character, 38–40, *43*;
    moral values, 33, 36, 41
evaluation, 8, 25, 45, 95, 137, 142, 144,
    174–75

fair play, *28*, 33, 43, 44, 46, 48, 101, 140
feedback, 48, 50–54, 56, 64, 76, 79–80,
    82, 87, 95, 122–*23*, *125*, 135–38,
    171–72;
    active listening, *59*, 60–62, 64;
    constructive, 56, 68–69, 72, 152;
    encouraging, 134;
    informational, 133–34;
    mistakes, 66, 68, 71–72, 74, 82, 91,
    112;
    observational, 123, 127, 154;
    peer, 152–54, 158;
    reciprocal style, 129;
    reinforcing, 134–35;
    timing of, 60, 115, 128, 145–47
formal learning, 163

game-based decision-making. *See*
    decision-making
games-based approach. *See* instructional
    styles
goals, 7, 14, 16, 23, 25–27, 58, 99, 103,
    113, 140–41, 145–46, 154, 174;
    goal setting, 78–80, 111, 113, *140*,
    147–48

harassment, 33, 84–86, 88, 95, 177
hazing, 36–37, 39, 84–86, 88, 90, 177
holistic athlete development, 9, 27–28,
    31–32, 53, 99, 104, 140

inclusion, *123*
inclusive practice, 7–8, 66–67, 74–75, 77,
    82, 84, 86, 91, 122, 129
individualization. *See* training principles
informal learning, 164, 175
injuries, 81, 83, 93, 105, 178
instructional styles, 17, 122–23, 125,
    130, 136–38;
    athlete-centered, 122–*23*;
    coach-centered, 122–*23*;

About the Authors

Pete Van Mullem is a professor in movement and sport sciences at Lewis-Clark State College (ID). He has more than 14 years of professional experience in coaching and athletic administrative positions at the middle school, high school, small college, and NCAA Division II and Division I levels. He serves on the editorial board for the *International Sport Coaching Journal* (ISCJ) and as managing editor for PHE (Physical & Health Education) America. Pete served as a member of the National Standards for Sport Coaches Revision Task Force for SHAPE (Society of Health and Physical Education) America. Pete received his doctorate in sport ethics from the University of Idaho, and his scholarly interests focus on coach development and ethical sport leadership. He has authored more than 40 articles related to coach development.

Lori Gano-Overway is an assistant professor and coaching education minor program director at James Madison University. She has been involved in coaching education for more than 20 years and conducts research on how the social psychological climate can be structured to provide positive experiences for young people and foster positive youth development. As an AASP-certified mental performance consultant she works with athletes on performance enhancement issues and collaborates with coaches on creating environments that foster positive experiences and performance enhancement outcomes for athletes. Lori serves on the editorial board of the the *Journal of*

Sport Psychology in Action, the *International Sport Coaching Journal,* and is the editor for the *Women in Sport and Physical Activity Journal.* She is a board member for the United States Center for Coaching Excellence and serves as their accreditation chair. Lori is also a member of the Virginia High School League coaching education committee and serves on the National Advisory Board for the Positive Coaching Alliance. She recently chaired the task force to revise the National Standards for Sport Coaches for SHAPE America.